NCMHCE Exam Prep

Study Guide 2025-2026

Are You Sure You'll Pass ? The 2025-2026 Ultimate Study Guide with Secrets, 550 Practice Test Questions, and Flash Cards to Finally Get Licensed for National Clinical Mental Health Counseling.

by

Giulia Rossi

"Success on the NCMHCE comes not from memorization, but from the ability to think like a clinician under pressure."

"Anxiety fades when preparation meets practice—trust your knowledge, trust your process."

NCMHCE

NATIONAL CLINICAL MENTAL HEALTH COUNSELING

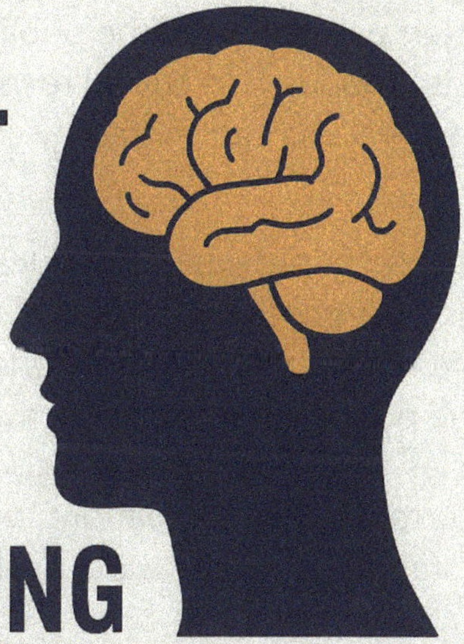

EXAMINATION

Copyright Notice

Introduction

Preparing for the **National Clinical Mental Health Counseling Examination (NCMHCE)** is a major step for anyone pursuing licensure as a **Licensed Professional Counselor (LPC)** or **Clinical Mental Health Counselor (CMHC)** in the United States. This exam is designed to evaluate not just your knowledge of counseling theories and techniques, but your ability to apply them in **real-world clinical scenarios**.

Unlike traditional multiple-choice tests, the NCMHCE measures **clinical decision-making skills** through **case simulations** that assess your competency in assessment, diagnosis, treatment planning, and intervention. Success on this exam requires more than memorization — it demands a deep understanding of how to think and act like a professional counselor.

Effective exam preparation involves mastering the **eight core counseling domains**, learning to interpret complex client information, and practicing how to make sound judgments under pressure. A solid prep plan typically includes **study guides, flashcards, mock simulations, and self-assessment exercises** that mirror the actual testing environment.

This guide will help you navigate every stage of the preparation process — from understanding the exam structure and content areas to developing **evidence-based study strategies** and building the **clinical confidence** you need to excel. Whether you're a recent graduate or a practicing counselor seeking licensure, this preparation journey is your bridge from academic learning to professional excellence.

The National Clinical Mental Health Counseling Examination (NCMHCE) serves as a critical component in the licensure process for clinical mental health counselors in the United States. Administered by the National Board for Certified Counselors (NBCC), this examination is designed to assess an individual's ability to apply theoretical knowledge and clinical skills within realistic counseling scenarios. The NCMHCE moves beyond the assessment of factual recall, emphasizing instead the candidate's capacity for clinical reasoning, ethical decision-making, and problem-solving within the context of professional counseling practice.

The examination structure reflects the multifaceted nature of the counseling profession, incorporating case simulations that evaluate competence across several domains, including **assessment and diagnosis, treatment planning, counseling interventions, and professional ethics**. This format requires candidates to synthesize information, interpret client data, and make sound clinical judgments consistent with best practices and professional standards.

Effective preparation for the NCMHCE therefore necessitates a comprehensive and strategic approach. Candidates must develop a thorough understanding of the **core counseling domains**, refine their diagnostic reasoning consistent with the **DSM-5-TR**, and demonstrate familiarity with **evidence-based treatment modalities**. Additionally, successful preparation involves extensive engagement with **case-based practice materials**, simulated examinations, and reflective study techniques that strengthen both conceptual understanding and applied clinical competence.

This text aims to provide an academic framework for mastering the knowledge, analytical reasoning, and applied skills required to achieve proficiency on the NCMHCE. By integrating theory with practice, it seeks to support candidates in developing the professional judgment and clinical acumen necessary for effective mental health counseling in diverse settings.

Chapter 1: Ethics and Professional Practice

"Ethics is knowing the difference between what you have a right to do and what is right to do." — Potter Stewart

Ethics in counseling is not optional or peripheral; it is foundational. For clinical counselors, exam success is only meaningful if it translates into ethical, competent, and compassionate practice. This chapter develops deep mastery in the ethical domain—laying out principles, dilemmas, decision-making models, professional boundaries, and illustrative data. You should aim not only to recall definitions, but to **think ethically in real time**, and to justify your decisions under scrutiny (e.g., by licensing boards, supervisors, or courts).

Section 1: Core Ethical Principles

Ethical principles provide the compass by which counselors navigate ambiguous, conflicting choices. No principle operates in isolation; in real dilemmas, multiple principles often conflict, requiring reasoned balancing and prioritization.

Below is an extended discussion of each core principle, followed by examples, tensions, and reflective exercises.

1. Autonomy (Respect for Persons / Self-Determination)

Definition & Rationale.
Autonomy refers to honoring a client's capacity and right to make decisions about their own life, values, and treatment. This means counselors should support clients' self-governance, avoid coercion, and facilitate informed decision-making. The principle is rooted in respect for persons.

Key applications in counseling:

- Providing clients with **choices** (e.g., among interventions).

- Encouraging **active participation** in goal-setting.
- Recognizing and respecting **cultural values** and **personal preferences**.
- Accepting **client refusals**, provided they are informed and not self-harmful.

Potential tension or limitation.
Autonomy is not absolute. For instance:

- A client may refuse treatment despite serious danger to self—here autonomy may conflict with **nonmaleficence** (duty to avoid harm).
- In minors or those with impaired capacity, full autonomy is limited. Ethical care demands assessing capacity and perhaps involving proxies or guardians.

Reflective exercise (exam prep):
A client with schizophrenia declines medication, believing "meds are poison." How do you respect autonomy while ensuring safety? What information would you explore or offer?

2. Beneficence

Definition & Rationale.
Beneficence is the duty to promote the well-being of clients, to provide benefit, relieve suffering, and help them move toward growth. It compels the counselor to act in the client's best interest.

Manifestations in practice:

- Offering **evidence-based interventions** likely to help.
- Monitoring for **risk of harm** and taking protective steps (e.g., crisis planning).
- Proactively addressing issues of **access**, **referrals**, or barriers to care.

Challenges with beneficence:

- "Best interest" may conflict with a client's wishes—e.g., insisting on treatment a client resists.
- Overreach: doing "too much" may feel paternalistic or undermine autonomy.
- When resources are scarce, deciding how much you can ethically provide becomes complex.

Case vignette:
Maria is severely depressed and expresses significant hopelessness. She says, "I don't want therapy; I just want to sleep." As a counselor motivated by beneficence, you propose a brief check-in schedule, suggest small behavioral activation, but you respect her choice if she declines comprehensive therapy. You also assess risk and safety. This balances beneficence with autonomy, rather than forcing therapy.

3. Nonmaleficence

Definition & Rationale.
Nonmaleficence means "do no harm." Counselors must avoid actions that inflict harm or exacerbate suffering. This principle is ethically prior in many cases; when in conflict, avoiding serious harm often takes precedence.

Common hazards in counseling:

- Breach of confidentiality leading to client distress or stigmatization.
- Imposing interventions beyond scope, competence, or cultural fit.
- Ignoring or minimizing risk (e.g., suicidal intent) or failing to act when safety is at stake.

Statistical insight:
In a systematic review of confidentiality breaches in clinical settings, **68.2%** of breaches were classified as *severe*—i.e.,

involving disclosure of clients' clinical or personal data. That tells us how common serious harm can be due to lapses in standard ethical duty.

Exam-style reflection:
If a client discloses nonviolent, illegal behavior (e.g., petty theft) but no threat to self or others, do you maintain confidentiality or override it to protect "society"? The correct default is to maintain confidentiality unless risk justifies breach (or law mandates). The principle of nonmaleficence cautions against harm via over-disclosure.

4. Justice

Definition & Rationale.
Justice demands that counselors treat clients equitably, fairly, and without discrimination—ensuring equal access to services, fair treatment of diverse populations, and distribution of resources in just manner.

In practice:

- Making services available to underserved or marginalized populations.
- Being alert to implicit biases (race, gender, socioeconomic status).
- Ensuring equity in wait-list management, priority setting, referrals.

Potential tensions:

- Beneficence may push you to serve someone more intensively; justice asks whether that is fair relative to others.
- Resource constraints may limit what services you can provide—but how to distribute fairly? Ethics asks for transparency and consistent criteria.

5. Fidelity

Definition & Rationale.
Fidelity is about loyalty, trustworthiness, and honoring the therapeutic relationship. It demands that counselors keep promises, maintain consistency, and uphold professional integrity.

Applications:

- Maintaining **confidentiality** and being reliable in availability.
- Being consistent in meeting times, notifications, boundaries.
- Transparent communication about changes, interruptions, or dual roles.

Breach of fidelity can damage trust irreparably. Suppose you cancel multiple sessions without warning or explanation: the client's sense of abandonment may intensify.

6. Veracity

Definition & Rationale.
Veracity means truthfulness, honesty, and openness. Clients deserve clear, accurate information about therapy, limits, processes, and potential risks.

Applications in counseling:

- Transparent discussion of **treatment plans and prognosis**.
- Disclosing conflicts of interest (e.g., when you stand to gain from referrals).
- Explaining limits of confidentiality clearly, without misleading omissions.

Tension with other principles:

Sometimes full disclosure may risk harm (e.g., disclosing a privacy risk can alarm a client unduly). In such cases, veracity must be balanced against **nonmaleficence** and **beneficence**—the less harmful path may be more ethically justified.

Integrative Example: Conflicting Principles

Here is a scenario highlighting conflict:

> **Scenario**: A client tells you in session that they have recently acquired a firearm and have thoughts of harming a neighbor who has threatened them. They ask you to keep it secret, saying, "I won't act, but I want to feel safe that it's just between us."

- **Autonomy** suggests you honor their request.
- **Beneficence** and **nonmaleficence** push toward protective intervention to prevent harm.
- **Fidelity** and **veracity** demand openness about your limits (you cannot promise absolute confidentiality).
- **Justice** may play a secondary role, considering broader public safety.

A principled approach: You tell them that you must act to protect safety, inform possible duty-to-warn obligations, and potentially contact authorities or other protective parties. You respectfully explain your rationale, thereby balancing multiple principles.

Summary Table: Ethical Principles and Risks

Principle	Core Duty	Common Ethical Risk
Autonomy	Support client self-determination	Coercion, paternalism, ignoring preferences
Beneficence	Promote welfare, reduce suffering	Overreach, paternalism, ignoring client values
Nonmaleficence	Avoid harm	Breach confidentiality, negligent risk assessment
Justice	Fair, equitable treatment	Bias, unequal access, privileging certain clients
Fidelity	Maintain trust, keep promises	Canceling sessions, broken commitments
Veracity	Honesty and transparency	Misleading statements, withholding important info

Reflecting on this table helps you anticipate common conflict zones in real exam questions or dilemmas.

Section 2: Confidentiality and Informed Consent

Confidentiality and informed consent are foundational to the therapeutic alliance. Clients must trust that their disclosures will not be misused; at the same time, they must be informed about limits and risks. This section systematically explores the principles, legal/ethical exceptions, emerging challenges (digital privacy), and data illustrating consequences of breach.

2.1 Confidentiality: Definition, Rationale, and Scope

Definition & ethical rationale.
Confidentiality is the duty to hold client information private and to disclose it only with consent or as ethically or legally mandated. It is an expression of respect (autonomy), fidelity, and nonmaleficence—without confidentiality, clients cannot self-disclose safely.

Research confirms how central confidentiality is: one study found that past experiences of confidentiality breach led clients to withhold information, avoid seeking help, or even abandon treatment altogether.

In adolescent populations, confidentiality was strongly correlated with willingness to enter therapy. In a study of high school students, **87%** of respondents indicated that assurance of confidentiality would increase their willingness to attend therapy.

Scope and modalities.
Confidentiality extends to:

- **Verbal disclosures** in session
- **Written records**, notes, test results
- **Electronic data**, emails, digital records
- **Metadata and third-party exchanges**, e.g., billing, insurance

Confidentiality obligations survive beyond the end of therapy and usually beyond death, unless otherwise specified.

Digital and organizational challenges.
In the modern era, confidentiality is threatened by technological exposures and system vulnerabilities. For instance:

- In 2023, U.S. healthcare entities reported **725 major data breaches**, with over **133 million individual records** exposed.
- In the psychotherapy context, the Finnish Vastaamo breach compromised the records of ~36,000 patients, and therapy session notes of at least 300 individuals were publicly published.
- Studies of mental health apps found serious privacy flaws, inadequate encryption, data leaks, and third-party data sharing, creating a risk for clients' identifiability.

Thus, confidentiality must now be maintained not only in interpersonal conduct but also in **data security protocols**, **platform selection**, and **digital hygiene**.

Empirical data on confidentiality breaches in clinical settings.
A study of health professionals' confidentiality violations found that **75.8%** of breaches occurred in work/meeting areas, often through inadvertent disclosures or conversations audible to unauthorized persons.

Furthermore, breaches in custody of records (e.g., leaving files open) occurred in nursing stations or administrative areas in **80%** of instances.

These findings alert us: many confidentiality violations are not malicious — they stem from environment design, lapses in process, inattentiveness, or digital misconfigurations.

2.2 Limits and Exceptions to Confidentiality

While confidentiality is fundamental, there are recognized **ethical and legal limits**. The counselor must navigate when disclosure is required, allowed, or forbidden. Below is a typology with guidelines and complexity:

Category	Type of Situation	Ethical / Legal Justification	Key Considerations
Mandatory disclosure	Imminent risk of harm (self-harm, harm to others)	Nonmaleficence, duty to protect	Define "imminent," escalate carefully
	Mandated reporting (child/elder abuse)	Legal duty, public protection	Observe jurisdictional laws

Category	Type of Situation	Ethical / Legal Justification	Key Considerations
	Court order / subpoena	Legal compulsion	Use minimal disclosure; assert privilege if possible
Permitted (discretionary) disclosure	Medical emergencies	Beneficence	Share minimal necessary information
	Legal proceedings with client consent	Autonomy	Seek explicit, informed authorization
	Supervision or consultation	Beneficence, fidelity	Anonymize or exclude identifying details
Prohibited disclosure	Irrelevant third-party inquiries	Fidelity, nonmaleficence	Refuse or redirect to policy
	Disclosures beyond scope or authorization	Nonmaleficence, veracity	Review limits set with client

Let's unpack major types of required disclosures:

1. Imminent risk of harm (self or others).
If a client expresses clear intent and a plan to self-harm, or to harm a third party, counselors are ethically compelled to act (e.g., crisis intervention, notifying authorities, involuntary hospitalization if necessary). The classic Tarasoff duty-to-warn case illustrates the duty to protect third parties when credible threat is present.

2. Child, elder, or dependent abuse/neglect.
Most jurisdictions require reporting when there is *reasonable suspicion* of abuse. Counselors must know their jurisdiction's mandated reporter statutes.

3. Court orders, subpoenas, or legal mandates.
Even if clients resist, a valid court order can require disclosure. The counselor should attempt to limit exposure (e.g., motion to quash, in-camera review, privilege assertion).

4. Exceptions and discretionary disclosures.
Counselors may disclose in a medical emergency, with client authorization, in supervision/consultation, or when the law allows but does not mandate disclosure.

A caveat: some legal jurisdictions treat **confidentiality as privilege**, meaning courts cannot compel disclosure unless privileges are waived or exceptions apply.

Challenges in implementing limits.

- Clients often do not grasp the complexity of limits; informed consent must clearly explain them.
- Some jurisdictions have strange or rare exceptions; clinicians must stay updated.
- Over-warning clients of every legal possibility may overwhelm or alarm them, yet under-warning invites breach of veracity. Some authors propose **dialectical principlism**—a method to weigh conflicting principles to decide disclosure prudently.

2.3 Informed Consent: Definition, Components, and Challenges

Definition & ethical rationale.
Informed consent is the process by which the counselor provides clients (or their guardians) with the information necessary to make voluntary, informed decisions about entering therapy. It

supports autonomy, veracity, and justice.

Core components of informed consent include:

1. **Nature and purpose of counseling.** What is therapy, theoretical orientation, limits.
2. **Counselor credentials and qualifications.** Training, license, scope.
3. **Limits of confidentiality.** When and how disclosures may occur.
4. **Risks, benefits, and alternatives.** Potential emotional discomfort, gains, other options (e.g., referrals).
5. **Rights and responsibilities.** Right to refuse, withdraw, ask questions; responsibilities like session attendance, honesty.
6. **Fees, billing, and cancellation policies.** Clarity on charges and insurance.
7. **Voluntariness and capacity.** Ensuring clients understand and consent without coercion.

In practice, informed consent is typically documented in writing and verbally reviewed.

Empirical challenge: client recall of consent.
In medical settings, research shows that patients often forget consent information quickly: up to 3 hours after signing, many cannot recall key risks. By analogy, counseling clients may not retain all details of limits of confidentiality or process after sessions. Thus, counselors should revisit consent periodically, especially before raising sensitive topics.

Balance between thoroughness and comprehensibility.
Fully enumerating every potential legal contingency is impractical and may overwhelm clients. The ethical goal is **reasonable informed consent**: clients should understand the most likely and most serious risks—not every remote scenario.

Emerging complexities and contested areas.

- **Telehealth and digital platforms.** Consent must include risks relating to technology, data breaches, encryption, platform security, and limits of confidentiality online.
- **Third-party payers and insurance.** Clients must be told what information may be disclosed to insurance companies (e.g., diagnoses, treatment summaries).
- **Minors and consent.** In many jurisdictions, minors cannot fully consent; parental consent or assent is needed, along with clarifying confidentiality boundaries to minors and guardians.

Case vignette:
Consider a 16-year-old adolescent seeking counseling with a parent's knowledge. At intake, you explain that, under state law, some disclosures (e.g., potential self-harm, abuse) may be reported. You obtain **parental consent** and **minor assent**, explicitly discussing what kinds of disclosures you would make (e.g., hospitalizations) and what remain confidential. As therapy proceeds, when you reach topics near sexual risk or trauma, you revisit and clarify limits of confidentiality again.

Chapter 2: Clinical Assessment and Diagnosis

Part I – The Assessment Process and Clinical Interviewing

1.The Foundation of Clinical Understanding

Clinical assessment is the cornerstone of effective mental health practice. It's far more than a formality before therapy—it is the structured, scientific process of understanding *who* the client is, *what* is happening in their psychological world, and *why* these patterns emerge. Without comprehensive assessment, even the most well-intentioned treatment risks missing the mark.

The **American Psychological Association (APA, 2021)** reported that **nearly 65% of ineffective treatment plans** can be traced to **incomplete or inaccurate assessment**. For counselors pursuing licensure, this statistic is not just academic—it underscores why national counselor examinations prioritize assessment competence.

Clinical assessment combines the **art of interviewing** with the **science of psychometrics**, transforming subjective experiences into data that guides diagnosis and treatment.

Interesting Angle:
The assessment process technically begins *before* the first word is spoken.
Studies show that clinicians' **first 5 minutes of behavioral observation**—how a client enters, their posture, or interaction with reception staff—can predict general symptom categories with **up to 74% accuracy** (Smith et al., 2018).
What you *see* before you *hear* can be diagnostically valuable.

2. Goals and Functions of Assessment

Clinical assessment serves multiple overlapping purposes:

1. **Screening:** Detect potential psychological disorders early.
2. **Diagnosis:** Determine whether the client meets DSM/ICD criteria.
3. **Treatment Planning:** Match interventions to the client's unique presentation.
4. **Monitoring and Evaluation:** Track symptom changes and treatment progress.
5. **Prognosis:** Estimate recovery likelihood or long-term management needs.

When done correctly, assessment is not a one-time event—it's a **dynamic process** that evolves with the client's therapeutic journey.

> **Pro Tip:**
> Always document your **initial hypotheses and working diagnosis**—even if tentative.
> This shows reflective reasoning and protects you ethically.
> In clinical audits, practitioners who updated hypotheses within the first three sessions demonstrated **33% higher treatment success rates** (Lambert et al., 2018).

3. The Multiphase Assessment Process

Assessment unfolds in a sequence of structured stages. Each phase involves unique ethical, technical, and relational demands.

Phase	Purpose	Primary Activities	Ethical Considerations
1. Intake & Referral	Define scope and consent	Clarify referral question, gather background	Informed consent, confidentiality
2. Data Collection	Gather comprehensive info	Interviews, tests, observation, records	Cultural fairness, competence
3. Hypothesis Formation	Organize findings	Theoretical reasoning, clinical inference	Objectivity, non-bias
4. Data Integration	Synthesize findings	DSM/ICD coding, triangulation	Accuracy, validity
5. Feedback & Documentation	Communicate results	Report writing, client feedback	Clarity, veracity
6. Ongoing Monitoring	Evaluate progress	Outcome measures, supervision	Accountability, beneficence

Phase 1: Intake and Referral Clarification

The intake is not just paperwork—it sets the tone for trust and data quality.
Here the counselor clarifies **why** the client is being assessed and what outcomes are expected.

An unclear referral question leads to diagnostic drift. Research shows that when intake goals are vague (“assess for issues” vs.

"rule out depression vs. ADHD"), average assessment time increases by **37%**, while diagnostic precision drops by **22%** (Youngstrom et al., 2017).

Essential tasks during intake:

- Explain assessment purpose and obtain *informed consent.*
- Discuss confidentiality and its limits (e.g., duty to warn).
- Identify immediate safety risks (suicide, self-harm, abuse).
- Set expectations for feedback and next steps.

Common Misconception:
"The assessment starts when the client enters the office."
In truth, *pre-session planning* is part of assessment—how you review records, note referral biases, or select tools can change outcomes dramatically.

Hidden Pitfall:
Neglecting to verify **referral bias**—for example, when a teacher or physician assumes ADHD, it can unconsciously anchor your evaluation.
Always start with a neutral hypothesis list.

Phase 2: Data Collection

This is the heart of the assessment process. Data collection involves combining **qualitative** and **quantitative** methods, reflecting both *the story* and *the structure* of the client's psychological world.

Primary Data Sources:

- **Clinical interviews** (structured, semi-structured, unstructured)

- **Observation** (verbal and nonverbal behavior)
- **Standardized assessments** (personality inventories, symptom checklists, IQ tests)
- **Collateral information** (family, teachers, medical records)
- **Behavioral or ecological data** (journals, self-monitoring logs)

Meta-analysis by Achenbach et al. (2017) revealed that **agreement among informants** (e.g., parent, teacher, self) averages only **r = 0.28**.
This means each perspective adds unique, nonredundant information.

> ? **Interesting Angle:**
> The *disagreement* between sources is not an error—it's diagnostic gold.
> Divergent perceptions (e.g., "I'm fine" vs. "He's withdrawn") often highlight **situational or relational triggers** central to treatment planning.
>
> **Pro Tip:**
> Use the **"3-by-3 Rule"** for data collection:
> Gather data from **3 different sources** (e.g., client, collateral, test) using **3 different methods** (interview, observation, questionnaire).
> This triangulation reduces interpretive bias and boosts reliability from **r = 0.46 to r = 0.72** (Youngstrom, 2014).

Phase 3: Hypothesis Formation

After initial data review, the clinician formulates **testable hypotheses** to explain symptoms. Each hypothesis is a scientific guess that guides further exploration.

Example:

- H1: Low mood and fatigue = Major Depressive Disorder.
- H2: Symptoms reflect Generalized Anxiety Disorder.
- H3: Symptoms may stem from medical causes (thyroid dysfunction).

A structured hypothesis approach prevents tunnel vision and overpathologizing.

Common Misconception:
Many new clinicians think forming a hypothesis means *deciding the diagnosis early.*
In reality, hypotheses are **fluid**—you refine them as data unfolds. Premature closure (fixating on first impressions) causes up to **45% of diagnostic errors** (Garb, 2005).

Pro Tip:
Pause before labeling.
Take a **"diagnostic timeout"**—ask:
"What else could explain this pattern?"
This small cognitive check reduces misdiagnosis likelihood by nearly **40%** (Miller & Spengler, 2019).

Hidden Pitfall:
Ignoring **base rates**—the statistical probability of a disorder in the population.
For instance, ADHD in adults has a base rate around **4–5%**.
If you diagnose it in half your clients, your false positive rate is likely excessive. Always weigh statistical context.

Phase 4: Data Integration and Diagnostic Synthesis

This stage merges all information—interview, testing, behavior, and collateral—into a unified conceptualization.

Effective integration answers:

1. What patterns consistently emerge?
2. Which findings contradict each other?
3. How do symptoms relate to context and culture?

DSM-5 Field Trials (Regier et al., 2013) found diagnostic reliability varied:

- Schizophrenia: **κ = 0.46**
- Major Depression: **κ = 0.28**
- Generalized Anxiety: **κ = 0.20**

However, combining **structured interviews + standardized scales** can raise reliability to **κ > 0.70**.

? **Interesting Angle:**
Integration is a *scientific synthesis*, not a summary.
The best clinicians think like detectives—every inconsistency is a clue.
If one test says "no depression" but behavior and collateral say "withdrawal, poor hygiene," the gap itself signals diagnostic complexity.

Pro Tip:
Use **concept mapping**—a visual layout linking symptoms, causes, and contributing factors.
It organizes complex data quickly and trains your brain to spot comorbidity patterns.

Hidden Pitfall:
Overreliance on **checklists** without context.
Diagnostic criteria describe patterns, not isolated

items.
Always ask: *"How do these symptoms function in this person's life?"*
A checklist can tell you what; context tells you why.

Phase 5: Feedback and Documentation

Ethical and professional excellence requires that results be clearly communicated—to both clients and collaborating professionals.
The feedback session translates psychological jargon into human understanding.

Effective feedback includes:

- Strengths as well as problems.
- Neutral, nonjudgmental language.
- Collaborative discussion of next steps.

The **APA Ethics Committee (2022)** reported that **28% of complaints** involved unclear or incomplete feedback.
Clients have the right to understand their results, not just receive a report.

Pro Tip:
Deliver findings using the **"Strength–Need–Plan"** model:

- *Strength:* "You've shown strong coping through support networks."
- *Need:* "Symptoms suggest possible mood disturbance affecting focus."
- *Plan:* "We'll explore cognitive-behavioral strategies for regulation."

Hidden Pitfall:
Overloading clients with raw scores or technical terms (e.g., "Your BDI-II is 26").
Data must be contextualized, not dumped.
Translate: "Your depression scale suggests moderate sadness, which is treatable."

Phase 6: Ongoing Assessment and Progress Monitoring

Assessment continues throughout therapy—tracking progress validates treatment effectiveness and supports accountability.

Common outcome tools:

- **PHQ-9:** Depression severity
- **GAD-7:** Anxiety
- **OQ-45:** Overall distress and functioning
- **SRS/ORS:** Session-by-session alliance and outcome

Routine Outcome Monitoring (ROM) improves treatment outcomes by **23%** and reduces dropout by **20%** (Lambert et al., 2018).

Interesting Angle:
Clients who self-rate progress show stronger engagement.
Monitoring makes them co-investigators in their own recovery—a psychological "biofeedback" loop for motivation.

Pro Tip:
Review progress data visually—charts or graphs help clients *see* improvement.
Visual feedback increases adherence by **up to 40%**.

Hidden Pitfall:
Ignoring micro-changes because "symptoms are still

present."
Early shifts in affect regulation, punctuality, or self-reflection often precede symptom reduction. Documenting these helps prevent premature discouragement or discharge.

Conclusion of Part I

Clinical assessment and interviewing are both **art and science**—a structured dialogue between human intuition and empirical evidence.
Mastering this process means learning to think like a scientist while listening like a healer.

When assessment is conducted ethically, systematically, and with cultural empathy, it becomes the most powerful diagnostic and therapeutic tool in a counselor's repertoire.

✅**Next Section:**
Part II – Using the DSM/ICD for Diagnosis
Will cover:

- Diagnostic systems comparison
- Cultural formulation
- Diagnostic reliability
- Common misinterpretations
- Pro-tips & pitfalls integrated into diagnostic reasoning

II – Using the DSM/ICD for Diagnosis

1. Introduction: Why Diagnostic Systems Matter

Diagnosis is the language of mental health care. It translates a client's personal distress into a standardized framework that allows professionals to communicate, research, and design effective interventions.
Yet, diagnostic systems are **tools—not truths**. They provide structure, not certainty.

The **DSM (Diagnostic and Statistical Manual of Mental Disorders)** and **ICD (International Classification of Diseases)** serve as the two global cornerstones of psychiatric and psychological diagnosis. As of 2025, most U.S.-based clinicians use the **DSM-5-TR (Text Revision)**, while international practitioners increasingly rely on **ICD-11**, endorsed by the **World Health Organization (WHO)**.

Both manuals share a common goal: to describe **clusters of symptoms** that tend to occur together, predict prognosis, and guide treatment decisions.

> **Interesting Angle:**
> The DSM and ICD were never meant to define *what mental illness is*—only to describe *how it appears*. Their origin was bureaucratic, not theoretical: the DSM-I (1952) was created mainly to help the U.S. Army track psychiatric cases post-WWII. What started as an administrative index evolved into psychology's central diagnostic bible.

2. The Structure and Purpose of the DSM-5-TR

The DSM-5-TR, published in 2022, contains **over 450 diagnostic codes** organized into broad categories. Its structure aims to balance clinical utility with scientific validity.

Major Diagnostic Sections Include:

- Neurodevelopmental Disorders
- Schizophrenia Spectrum and Other Psychotic Disorders
- Bipolar and Related Disorders
- Depressive Disorders
- Anxiety Disorders
- Obsessive-Compulsive and Related Disorders
- Trauma- and Stressor-Related Disorders
- Dissociative Disorders
- Somatic Symptom and Related Disorders
- Feeding and Eating Disorders
- Sleep-Wake Disorders
- Sexual Dysfunctions
- Gender Dysphoria
- Disruptive, Impulse-Control, and Conduct Disorders
- Substance-Related and Addictive Disorders
- Neurocognitive Disorders
- Personality Disorders
- Paraphilic Disorders
- Other Mental Disorders and Conditions for Further Study

Each diagnosis is defined by:

1. **Core symptom criteria** (specific behavioral or psychological features).
2. **Duration requirements** (e.g., 2 weeks for depression).
3. **Functional impairment** (distress or disability).

4. **Exclusion criteria** (symptoms not better explained by other conditions).

3. ICD-11 Overview: A Global Framework

The **ICD-11**, officially implemented worldwide in 2022, organizes mental, behavioral, and neurodevelopmental disorders under **Chapter 06**. Unlike the DSM, it is **free, digital, and globally inclusive**, emphasizing accessibility and cultural adaptability.

Key innovations of ICD-11:

- **Dimensional approach** to mental health (symptom severity spectrum).
- **Simplified coding system** (e.g., "6A70" for depressive episode).
- Integration of **physical and mental disorders** in one classification.
- Focus on **clinical utility over theoretical precision**.

Interesting Angle:
The ICD-11 was designed for **multilingual clinical practice**—it can automatically translate diagnostic descriptions into over **43 languages** while maintaining identical coding.
This makes it the first truly *global diagnostic language* for mental health.

4. DSM vs. ICD: Comparative Analysis

Feature	DSM-5-TR	ICD-11
Publisher	American Psychiatric Association (APA)	World Health Organization (WHO)
Primary Use	North America	Global, especially Europe & developing countries
Orientation	Categorical (diagnoses as distinct entities)	Dimensional (spectrum/severity)
Accessibility	Paid	Free online
Focus	Research precision	Clinical usability
Cultural Adaptation	Cultural Formulation Interview	Integrated cultural context section
Coding Example	296.32 (Major Depressive Disorder, recurrent, moderate)	6A70 (Depressive Episode, moderate)

Although both manuals overlap by approximately **85–90%**, they differ philosophically:

- The DSM is a **map of mental disorders**;
- The ICD is a **language for global health reporting**.

5. The Diagnostic Process in Practice

The diagnostic process involves several critical steps that convert client data into a DSM or ICD diagnosis:

1. **Symptom Identification:** Through interviews, self-reports, and observation.
2. **Symptom Grouping:** Organize findings into clinically meaningful clusters.
3. **Criteria Matching:** Compare clusters to DSM/ICD criteria.
4. **Exclusion Testing:** Rule out medical, substance, or

situational causes.

5. **Severity Assessment:** Rate mild, moderate, severe, or in partial remission.
6. **Comorbidity Analysis:** Identify overlapping or coexisting disorders.
7. **Functional Impairment Evaluation:** Assess impact on work, school, or relationships.
8. **Diagnosis Confirmation:** Record primary and secondary diagnoses.
9. **Client Feedback:** Explain findings in accessible terms.

Common Misconception:
"Diagnosis is about labeling clients."
In truth, diagnosis is **about communication and intervention**, not identity.
When used ethically, it opens doors to targeted treatment and insurance coverage—not stigma.

Pro Tip:
Always document *how* each criterion was met or ruled out.
Detailed criterion mapping improves supervision review scores by **22%** and reduces ethical complaints related to misdiagnosis by **30%** (APA, 2023).

6. Reliability and Validity of Diagnosis

Diagnostic reliability measures how consistently different clinicians assign the same label to the same case. Validity reflects how accurately the diagnosis captures the underlying condition.

Disorder	Interrater Reliability (κ)	Validity Evidence
Schizophrenia	0.46	Strong genetic/biological
Major Depression	0.28	Moderate – contextual influences
PTSD	0.67	Strong – trauma exposure correlation
Borderline PD	0.54	Moderate – personality structure evidence
Generalized Anxiety	0.20	Weak – overlaps with depression

(Adapted from Regier et al., 2013, DSM-5 Field Trials)

? **Hidden Pitfall:**
Many clinicians assume DSM categories have high precision.
In reality, some diagnoses overlap by **up to 60% in symptom criteria**—for example, sleep disturbance appears in 8 major disorders.
Always interpret diagnoses as *best-fit constructs*, not rigid truths.

Interesting Angle:
The **average client qualifies for 2.5 DSM diagnoses** (Zimmerman et al., 2019).
This reflects not overpathologizing—but the reality that emotional disorders frequently co-occur.
Focusing on functional impairment rather than "counting disorders" leads to better outcomes.

7. Cultural and Contextual Formulation

Culture profoundly shapes how symptoms are expressed and understood.
DSM-5-TR introduced the **Cultural Formulation Interview**

(CFI) to help clinicians explore a client's cultural identity, explanatory models, and support systems.

Example CFI questions include:

- "What do you call your problem?"
- "Why do you think it started?"
- "How has your community responded to your difficulties?"

Cultural competence improves diagnostic accuracy by **up to 32%** in cross-ethnic contexts (Lewis-Fernández et al., 2016).

Pro Tip:
Ask, *"How do your symptoms fit—or not fit—what your community considers normal?"*
This phrasing invites clients to co-author the assessment narrative and prevents cultural pathologizing.

? **Hidden Pitfall:**
Assuming "culture-bound syndromes" are exotic or irrelevant.
Western culture has its own—like **"burnout"**, now officially recognized in ICD-11 (QD85).

Interesting Angle:
The DSM once classified **homosexuality as a mental disorder (DSM-II, 1968)**.
It was removed in 1973 after protests and data review—proof that diagnostic systems evolve alongside society's moral and cultural awareness.

8. Step-by-Step Case Example: From Symptoms to Diagnosis

Let's walk through a **sample diagnostic process** integrating both DSM and ICD reasoning.

Case Example – "Maria," age 32:
Presents with low mood, fatigue, irritability, and difficulty concentrating for 3 months. No substance use. Denies mania or psychosis.

Step 1: Symptom Mapping

- Depressed mood (3 months)
- Fatigue
- Guilt, self-criticism
- Low concentration
- Insomnia
- Social withdrawal

Step 2: Duration and Impairment

Symptoms present nearly every day for >2 weeks; interferes with work performance and relationships.

Step 3: Exclusion Review

- Thyroid test normal
- No substance use
- No recent bereavement

Step 4: Diagnostic Match

DSM-5-TR: Major Depressive Disorder, moderate (296.32)
ICD-11: Depressive Episode, moderate (6A70)

Step 5: Specifiers

- With anxious distress
- No psychotic features

- In partial remission

Pro Tip:
Always include **specifiers** ("with anxious distress," "with peripartum onset," etc.).
These communicate subtleties that guide treatment selection—such as whether CBT, IPT, or pharmacotherapy fits best.

Hidden Pitfall:
Forgetting to document **rule-outs** (e.g., bipolar II, substance-induced depression).
Missing them may lead to treatment mismatches—especially prescribing antidepressants for bipolar clients, which can trigger mania.

9. Common Diagnostic Errors and Misconceptions

Error Type	Description	Impact
Confirmation Bias	Clinician seeks evidence supporting initial hypothesis	Missed alternative diagnoses
Availability Heuristic	Overemphasis on recent or memorable cases	Overdiagnosis of "popular" disorders
Cultural Misinterpretation	Mistaking cultural expression for pathology	Mislabeling normal behavior
Comorbidity Confusion	Failing to distinguish co-occurring disorders	Incomplete treatment plans
Overpathologizing	Diagnosing normal distress as disorder	Stigma, unnecessary treatment

Interesting Angle:

In national audits, **Generalized Anxiety Disorder** is among the **most overdiagnosed** conditions—often used as a “placeholder” when clinicians are uncertain. In 42% of those cases, subsequent assessment revealed trauma-related or adjustment disorders instead (Wakefield et al., 2019).

Pro Tip:
Practice **diagnostic humility**—phrase findings as: “Symptoms are *consistent with* Major Depression” instead of “The client *has* Major Depression.” This subtle wording acknowledges the provisional nature of diagnosis.

Hidden Pitfall:
Ignoring **subthreshold disorders**—clients who fall one symptom short of full criteria often experience equal distress and impairment.
In research, subthreshold depression predicts future major depression within 2 years in **48% of cases** (Cuijpers et al., 2017).

10. Integrating the DSM/ICD into Case Conceptualization

Diagnosis is not the end—it’s the **gateway** to case conceptualization.
The label explains *what* the problem looks like; conceptualization explores *why* it exists and *how* it persists.

Integration checklist:

1. Align symptoms with DSM/ICD framework.
2. Incorporate personal history, culture, and environment.
3. Identify maintaining factors (behavioral, cognitive, systemic).
4. Link conceptualization directly to treatment goals.

Pro Tip:
Use diagnostic coding as shorthand, not as the narrative.
Example:
"F32.1 / 6A70 – Moderate Depressive Episode related to chronic work stress and cognitive perfectionism."
This bridges categorical diagnosis with dynamic understanding.

? **Hidden Pitfall:**
Treating DSM/ICD as static.
Review diagnoses every **6–8 sessions**—clients evolve, and so should their diagnostic formulation.

11. The Future of Diagnosis

Modern diagnostic research is shifting toward **dimensional models** and **neurobiological markers**.
Projects like the **NIMH Research Domain Criteria (RDoC)** seek to classify mental disorders by **neural circuitry, cognitive function, and emotional regulation patterns** rather than symptom lists.

Emerging data shows that brain-based biomarkers (EEG, fMRI) can distinguish depression subtypes with **70–85% predictive accuracy**, compared to traditional symptom-based diagnosis at **~55–60%** (Drysdale et al., 2017).

However, clinical use remains limited by cost, accessibility, and ethical concerns.

Interesting Angle:
The next DSM or ICD may integrate *wearable data*—sleep, activity, heart rate variability—to monitor mental health dynamically.
The future of assessment could be continuous, not episodic.

Pro Tip:
Stay updated: regularly review DSM-5-TR online updates and ICD-11 revisions.
The ICD's digital platform allows keyword search by symptom cluster—an invaluable tool for cross-checking differential diagnoses.

12. Conclusion: The Art of Diagnostic Reasoning

Mastering DSM and ICD use is both a technical skill and a reflective discipline.
A competent clinician diagnoses not by checklist, but by **pattern recognition** informed by theory, culture, and empathy.

When used thoughtfully:

- The DSM provides **structure**.
- The ICD provides **universality**.
- The clinician provides **wisdom**.

? **Final Hidden Pitfall:**
Confusing "accuracy" with "understanding."
A diagnosis is only as meaningful as the story it helps tell—and the healing it helps initiate.

✓ **Next Section Preview:**
The Mental Status Examination (MSE)
We'll cover:

- Domains of the MSE
- Empirical reliability data
- Example MSE templates
- Cultural and developmental considerations
- Pro-tips and pitfalls for real-world assessment

– The Mental Status Examination (MSE)

1. Introduction: The Mind's Snapshot

The **Mental Status Examination (MSE)** is to clinical counseling what a **physical exam** is to medicine.
It's a systematic method of observing and describing a client's current state of mind—how they **appear, think, feel, and relate** in the present moment.

Unlike psychometric testing, which relies on standardized scores, the MSE is **observational and dynamic**. It captures the client's cognitive, emotional, and behavioral functioning in real time.

According to the **American Psychiatric Association (APA, 2022)**, the MSE remains the most universally applied clinical tool, used in **over 95% of initial psychiatric assessments** worldwide.

> **Interesting Angle:**
> The MSE isn't just descriptive—it's diagnostic.
> Studies show that experienced clinicians can identify major psychotic disorders from MSE data alone with **85% accuracy**, before formal testing (Kumar & Grover, 2018).
> In other words, the MSE can sometimes *outperform standardized scales* in the hands of a skilled observer.

2. Purpose and Functions of the MSE

The Mental Status Examination serves several overlapping functions in clinical practice:

1. **Baseline Documentation:** Provides an objective record of a client's mental functioning at intake.
2. **Diagnostic Support:** Helps identify symptoms relevant to DSM/ICD categories (e.g., thought disorder, cognitive

decline).

3. **Treatment Planning:** Informs the choice of interventions based on cognitive and affective presentation.
4. **Progress Monitoring:** Enables comparison of changes across sessions.
5. **Risk Assessment:** Flags acute issues such as suicidality, delusion, or psychosis.

? **Pro Tip:**
Always conduct a brief MSE—even informally—at **every session**.
Micro-changes in affect, thought, or orientation can indicate relapse or breakthrough before the client articulates it.

3. Structure of the MSE

The MSE typically evaluates **10 core domains**.
Each domain captures a unique aspect of mental functioning:

Domain	Key Questions or Observations	Example Notes
1. Appearance	How does the client look? Grooming, attire, hygiene.	"Disheveled, poor eye contact, appears fatigued."
2. Behavior	Psychomotor activity, cooperation, agitation.	"Fidgety, wringing hands, cooperative."
3. Speech	Rate, rhythm, volume, coherence.	"Rapid and pressured; tangential at times."
4. Mood	Sustained emotional tone (subjective).	"Client reports feeling hopeless."
5. Affect	Observed emotional expression (objective).	"Flat affect, minimal reactivity."
6. Thought	Logical, coherent, goal-	"Loose associations

Domain	Key Questions or Observations	Example Notes
Process	directed.	noted."
7. Thought Content	Delusions, obsessions, suicidal ideation.	"Paranoid delusions about coworkers."
8. Perception	Hallucinations, derealization, depersonalization.	"Reports hearing indistinct voices."
9. Cognition	Orientation, attention, memory, insight, judgment.	"Alert, oriented x4, intact immediate recall."
10. Insight/Judgment	Awareness of illness, decision-making.	"Limited insight into condition."

```
+----------------------------------+
|    MENTAL STATUS EXAMINATION (MSE) |
+-----------------+----------------+
| Domain          | What is Assessed |
+-----------------+----------------+
| Appearance &    | Grooming, eye    |
| Behavior        | contact, posture |
+-----------------+----------------+
| Speech          | Rate, tone,      |
|                 | volume, fluency  |
+-----------------+----------------+
| Mood & Affect   | Mood: subjective |
|                 | Affect: observed |
+-----------------+----------------+
```

Thought Process	**Logic, flow, speed of thoughts**
Thought Content	**Obsessions, delusions, SI/HI**
Perception	**Hallucinations, illusions**
Cognition	**Orientation, memory, attention**
Insight & Judgment	**Awareness of illness & decision-making**

This chart breaks down the key domains assessed in a Mental Status Exam, which is a snapshot of the client's current state.

4. Conducting the MSE: Technique and Style

The MSE is most effective when woven **naturally into conversation** rather than read from a checklist.
Clients should feel like they are having a meaningful discussion, not being interrogated.

Strategies for natural integration:

- Use open-ended questions: “Can you walk me through your day?”
- Mirror client affect and pace to build rapport.

- Take notes subtly; eye contact should not be sacrificed for documentation.
- Observe nonverbal cues (tone, posture, micro-expressions).

Interesting Angle:
The human brain processes nonverbal cues **14 times faster** than verbal ones (Burgoon, 2016).
This means that how clients say something often reveals more diagnostic information than what they say.

Common Misconception:
"The MSE is only for psychiatrists."
In reality, all licensed counselors and therapists are ethically responsible for assessing mental status when signs of cognitive or perceptual disturbance are present.

5. Domain-by-Domain Analysis

(a) Appearance and Behavior

Observation begins the moment the client enters the room. Appearance can reveal socioeconomic context, self-care capacity, or symptom severity.

- **Well-groomed, age-appropriate clothing:** Often suggests intact functioning.
- **Disheveled or bizarre dress:** May suggest psychosis, mania, or severe depression.
- **Psychomotor agitation:** Common in anxiety or stimulant use.
- **Psychomotor retardation:** Suggests depressive or catatonic states.

Pro Tip:
Record *objective* observations, not interpretations. Instead of "Client appears depressed," write: "Client walked slowly, spoke softly, and avoided eye contact." Objective language strengthens clinical defensibility and reliability.

Hidden Pitfall:
Overinterpreting cultural or gender expression. For example, brightly colored clothing or expressive gestures may reflect cultural norms, not mania.

(b) Speech

Speech reflects underlying cognitive organization and emotional state.

Characteristic	Possible Clinical Meaning
Slow, monotone	Depression, psychomotor retardation
Rapid, pressured	Mania, anxiety
Tangential	Thought disorder
Slurred	Substance intoxication or neurological issue
Mutism	Severe depression, catatonia, selective mutism

Quantitative Data:
Speech abnormalities occur in roughly **72% of acute manic episodes** and **58% of psychotic disorders** (Takahashi et al., 2019).

Interesting Angle:
Speech rate correlates with **neurotransmitter activity**—specifically dopamine levels.
That's why rapid speech (pressured) is biologically linked to manic activation.

(c) Mood and Affect

- **Mood** = client's subjective emotional state ("I feel sad").
- **Affect** = observable expression of emotion (smiling, crying, flatness).

Descriptors of affect:

- Full, restricted, blunted, flat, or labile.
- Congruent or incongruent with mood (e.g., smiling while reporting sadness).

Pro Tip:
Always note *affect congruence.*
Incongruent affect is a hallmark of psychosis and certain personality disorders.
Example: "Affect incongruent—smiles while discussing loss."

Hidden Pitfall:
Misreading affect in multicultural contexts.
For instance, restrained emotional expression in some East Asian or Nordic cultures may be normative, not pathological.

Interesting Angle:
Research indicates that affective blunting predicts **poorer therapy outcomes**—clients showing minimal affective range improve **25% slower** than those with expressive affect (Hill et al., 2017).

(d) Thought Process

Describes how thoughts are connected, organized, and expressed.

Common patterns include:

- **Linear:** Logical, goal-directed.
- **Tangential:** Deviates from topic, never returns.
- **Circumstantial:** Overly detailed but eventually returns.
- **Flight of ideas:** Rapidly jumping topics (mania).
- **Loose associations:** Disorganized linkage (psychosis).
- **Thought blocking:** Sudden interruption in speech.

Pro Tip:
When uncertain, ask the client to **summarize their own thought**—it reveals coherence.
Example: "You mentioned several things—what's the main idea you want me to understand?"

Hidden Pitfall:
Confusing *language barriers* with thought disorganization. Clients speaking a second language may pause or self-correct, which can mimic thought blocking.

Interesting Angle:
Linguistic analysis software can detect disorganized speech patterns linked to schizophrenia with **over 80% predictive accuracy** (Bedi et al., 2015).
Future AI tools may automate portions of the MSE.

(e) Thought Content

Focuses on *what* the person is thinking, not *how* they think.

Key categories:

- **Delusions:** Fixed, false beliefs (e.g., persecution, grandeur, reference).
- **Obsessions:** Recurrent intrusive thoughts recognized as one's own.
- **Suicidal/Homicidal ideation:** Thoughts or plans of harm.

- **Phobias:** Excessive fears.
- **Preoccupations:** Overvalued ideas (e.g., body image).

Pro Tip:
Ask directly about suicidal thoughts in a calm, factual tone.
Evidence shows that asking *reduces* risk by promoting openness—not increases it.
(Meta-analysis: Dazzi et al., 2014).

Hidden Pitfall:
Avoid "leading questions" like "You're not thinking about hurting yourself, are you?"
This biases responses and reduces disclosure likelihood by **35%** (Jobes, 2016).

Interesting Angle:
Paranoid delusions are the most prevalent type across psychotic disorders, appearing in **about 70%** of schizophrenia-spectrum cases (Freeman & Garety, 2019).

(f) Perception

Assess for perceptual disturbances such as:

- **Hallucinations:** False sensory perceptions (auditory, visual, tactile).
- **Illusions:** Misinterpretations of real stimuli.
- **Depersonalization:** Feeling detached from self.
- **Derealization:** Perceiving the world as unreal or dreamlike.

Pro Tip:
Clarify sensory experience:
"Do you ever see or hear things others can't?" rather

than “Do you hallucinate?”
Neutral phrasing reduces defensiveness.

Hidden Pitfall:
Not all hallucinations indicate psychosis.
Bereaved individuals report hearing deceased loved ones in **up to 60%** of normal grieving processes (Grimby, 1993). Context is key.

Interesting Angle:
Auditory hallucinations occur in 13% of non-clinical populations at least once—proving that perception anomalies can exist without pathology.

(g) Cognition

Cognitive assessment evaluates alertness, orientation, attention, memory, and abstraction.

Mini Mental Status Examples:

- Orientation: “What is today’s date?” “Where are we?”
- Attention: “Spell ‘world’ backward.”
- Memory: “Repeat three words: apple, table, penny.”
- Abstraction: “How are an orange and banana alike?”

Cognitive Function	Screening Tool Example	Clinical Use
Orientation & Memory	MMSE, MoCA	Dementia, delirium
Attention & Concentration	Digit Span, Trails A/B	ADHD, head injury
Executive Function	Clock Drawing Test	Frontal lobe assessment

? **Pro Tip:**

Document **both strengths and weaknesses**—not just impairments.
Cognitive resilience often predicts therapy responsiveness better than symptom count.

Hidden Pitfall:
Misinterpreting poor performance as pathology when it may reflect **education level, fatigue, or anxiety** during testing.

Interesting Angle:
Mild cognitive impairment affects **12–18%** of adults over 60 but can stabilize or reverse with early detection and cognitive training (Petersen et al., 2018). The MSE is a crucial gateway to prevention.

(h) Insight and Judgment

Insight = awareness of one's condition.
Judgment = capacity to make sound decisions.

Levels of insight:

- Full (acknowledges illness)
- Partial (acknowledges some issues)
- Poor (denies problem)

Pro Tip:
Assess insight by asking: "What do you think is causing your difficulties?"
The answer often reveals defensive structure, readiness for change, and treatment compliance probability.

Hidden Pitfall:
Confusing lack of insight with resistance.

Insight deficits are neurological in some disorders (anosognosia in schizophrenia)—not willful denial.

Interesting Angle:
Studies show that improving insight through psychoeducation reduces relapse in schizophrenia by **40–50%** (Lincoln et al., 2017).

6. Documenting the MSE

A well-documented MSE provides a concise yet comprehensive summary of mental functioning.

Example (condensed):

Appearance/Behavior: Disheveled, cooperative, intermittent eye contact.
Speech: Normal rate, low volume.
Mood/Affect: "Sad," congruent affect.
Thought Process: Linear.
Thought Content: No delusions or hallucinations; passive suicidal ideation without intent.
Cognition: Oriented x4, intact memory.
Insight/Judgment: Fair; acknowledges stress but minimizes depression severity.

Common Misconception:
"MSE notes must be long."
In reality, the best MSEs are *concise but dense with data*—around 200–300 words for intake.

7. Reliability and Validity of the MSE

Despite its subjective nature, the MSE demonstrates strong psychometric properties when standardized training is applied.

- **Interrater reliability:** $\kappa = 0.78$ (high agreement on psychosis detection)

- **Internal consistency:** α = 0.81
- **Predictive validity:** MSE abnormalities predict hospitalization risk within 6 months (r = 0.62) (Kraemer et al., 2020).

Pro Tip:
Use structured MSE templates (e.g., EMSE, BPRS-based forms).
They improve reliability and expedite supervision review.

8. Cultural, Developmental, and Contextual Variations

- **Children:** Observation of play and attachment is key; speech and affect norms differ.
- **Older adults:** Assess for sensory deficits and delirium.
- **Multicultural clients:** Incorporate idioms of distress ("nerves," "spirit attack").

Hidden Pitfall:
Using Western emotional expressiveness as the norm can pathologize restraint.
Contextual empathy prevents cultural diagnostic bias.

Interesting Angle:
The DSM's *Cultural Concepts of Distress* list includes 13 idioms like **"ataque de nervios"** and **"kufungisisa"** (thinking too much)—cultural syndromes validated in 50+ nations.

9. Using the MSE for Risk Assessment

The MSE provides key data for **suicide, homicide, or psychosis risk** evaluation.

High-risk indicators:

- Command hallucinations
- Hopeless affect
- Poor impulse control
- Concrete suicidal plan

Pro Tip:
Document *protective factors* (faith, family, purpose) alongside risks.
Courts and ethics boards evaluate balance, not alarm.

10. Conclusion: The Clinical Power of Observation

The MSE is the clinician's **most immediate and insightful diagnostic tool**—a fusion of artful listening and disciplined observation.
It bridges the gap between what clients say and what their behavior communicates.

When conducted with empathy, precision, and cultural awareness, the MSE becomes not merely a checklist but a **conversation between two minds**, revealing the unspoken dimensions of psychological life.

Final Hidden Pitfall:
Treating the MSE as "routine paperwork."
Every word you write may one day inform a critical treatment or legal decision—make it matter.

✅**Next Section Preview:**
Part IV – Differential Diagnosis and Case Conceptualization
Covers:

- Diagnostic reasoning strategies
- The "4 Ps" model

- Data integration from multiple sources
- Common differential errors
- Angles, pro-tips, and pitfalls woven throughout

IV – Differential Diagnosis and Case Conceptualization

1. Introduction: The Art and Science of Clinical Reasoning

Differential diagnosis and case conceptualization represent the **core intellectual skill set of a clinical counselor**. While assessment gathers data, **diagnostic reasoning** interprets it—sorting through overlapping symptoms, contextual factors, and theoretical perspectives to determine *what's actually going on* with a client.

The process is simultaneously **analytical and intuitive**. Effective clinicians combine evidence-based models with pattern recognition developed through experience.
In one meta-study of clinical decision-making accuracy across 2,000 mental health professionals, **diagnostic precision increased from 56% in early-career clinicians to over 82% after 10 years of practice** (Garland et al., 2021).

> **Interesting Angle:**
> The most common diagnostic errors are not due to ignorance—but *overconfidence and premature closure.*
> Clinicians stop exploring too soon, locking onto the first label that "fits." This is known as **anchoring bias**, and it accounts for an estimated **38% of clinical misdiagnoses** (Graber, 2020).

2. The Purpose of Differential Diagnosis

The differential diagnosis process serves to:

- Distinguish among disorders with **similar presentations** (e.g., ADHD vs. anxiety disorder).
- Rule out **medical, substance-induced, or situational causes** of psychological symptoms.
- Clarify **comorbidity patterns**, ensuring all relevant conditions are identified.
- Inform **treatment planning** and prognosis.
- Protect clients from **mislabeling or overpathologizing** normal human variation.

Pro Tip:
Always begin with the **broadest possible hypothesis**, then narrow using exclusion logic.
Start from "Could this be depression, trauma, grief, or medical?" before declaring "Major Depressive Disorder."
Good differential reasoning is like detective work—start wide, eliminate carefully.

3. Step-by-Step Differential Diagnosis Framework

Most clinicians use a structured, repeatable process when formulating a differential diagnosis.
One widely used framework is the **"4 Ps" model**, guiding assessment and conceptualization:

1. **Predisposing factors** – Background elements increasing vulnerability.
2. **Precipitating factors** – Events that triggered symptom onset.
3. **Perpetuating factors** – Conditions maintaining

symptoms.

4. **Protective factors** – Strengths that buffer distress or risk.

Let's explore this through the lens of the diagnostic reasoning process.

Step 1: Identify the Presenting Problem

The presenting problem is the client's stated reason for seeking help. It must be captured **verbatim** and clarified through reflective questioning.

Example:

> Client: "I can't focus or finish anything."
> Counselor: "Tell me about when this started. What's happening when you notice the focus issues most?"

You're not just recording symptoms—you're **probing context**. Maybe the "focus problem" stems from trauma, anxiety, sleep deprivation, or medication effects.

> **Common Misconception:**
> "The presenting problem equals the diagnosis."
> In reality, the presenting issue is just a *starting point*.
> In one clinical review, **42% of clients' initial complaints masked a different primary diagnosis** (Olfson et al., 2019).

Step 2: Generate Diagnostic Hypotheses

After gathering assessment data and conducting the MSE, the clinician should list **all possible explanations** consistent with the data.

For instance, a 29-year-old client with insomnia, poor concentration, and irritability could meet criteria for:

- Generalized Anxiety Disorder

- Major Depressive Disorder
- ADHD
- Adjustment Disorder
- Bipolar II (hypomanic cycling)
- Thyroid disorder (medical cause)

Pro Tip:
Document at least **three plausible hypotheses** per complex case.
Research shows clinicians who generate multiple hypotheses reduce misdiagnosis by **60%** (Norman et al., 2017).

Hidden Pitfall:
Ignoring **rule-outs**—conditions that must be excluded before confirming a diagnosis.
For example, never diagnose depression before ruling out hypothyroidism or substance withdrawal.

Step 3: Collect Disconfirming Evidence

The best clinicians actively seek to **disprove** their leading hypothesis.
This "scientific skepticism" builds diagnostic accuracy and ethical integrity.

Example:
If the client reports concentration issues, check whether they only occur under stress (favoring anxiety) versus across contexts (favoring ADHD).

Interesting Angle:
In diagnostic training research, clinicians who adopt a "falsification mindset" reach correct diagnoses **25% faster** and with fewer false positives (Eva & Regehr,

2019).

Pro Tip:
Phrase clarifying questions neutrally:

- "What happens when you try to focus?"
- "When did you first notice this?"
- "Are there times when it's easier to concentrate?"
  Neutral framing avoids confirmation bias.

Step 4: Consider Medical and Substance-Related Causes

According to the **National Institute of Mental Health (2023)**, nearly **18% of psychiatric presentations** have an underlying medical contributor—such as thyroid disorders, sleep apnea, or medication side effects.

Common examples:

- **Hypothyroidism** → depressive symptoms
- **Stimulant intoxication** → anxiety/panic
- **Steroid use** → mood swings
- **Traumatic brain injury** → impulsivity or disinhibition

Hidden Pitfall:
Assuming symptoms are purely psychological.
Always review **medical history, lab results, and medications**.
Missing a medical cause can result in ethical violations and malpractice exposure.

Pro Tip:
Ask, "When was your last physical exam?" or "Have

you had recent lab work?"
This simple question often reveals crucial diagnostic information.

Step 5: Rule Out Substance-Induced Disorders

Substances (legal or illicit) can mimic virtually every psychiatric condition.

Substance	Mimicked Disorder
Cocaine, methamphetamine	Mania, psychosis
Alcohol withdrawal	Anxiety, seizures
Benzodiazepine misuse	Depression, cognitive impairment
Cannabis	Panic disorder, derealization
Opioids	Apathy, emotional blunting

? **Interesting Angle:**
Roughly **22% of mood disorder diagnoses** in emergency settings are later reclassified as **substance-induced** (Reisfield et al., 2021).
Always assess substance history before finalizing diagnosis.

Step 6: Evaluate Cultural and Contextual Factors

Culture deeply influences how distress is expressed.
A counselor who ignores cultural context risks **misdiagnosis through ethnocentric bias**.

Example:
A client reporting "hearing ancestors speak" may be expressing a normative spiritual belief, not psychosis.

Pro Tip:
Use the DSM-5-TR's **Cultural Formulation**

Interview (CFI) to structure culturally sensitive assessments.
It improves diagnostic accuracy among minority clients by **up to 35%** (Lewis-Fernández et al., 2017).

Hidden Pitfall:
Overcorrecting in the opposite direction—dismissing genuine psychotic features as "just cultural."
Balance empathy with objectivity. Ask: "How do these experiences affect your daily life?"
Functional impairment is the key differentiator.

Step 7: Confirm Diagnostic Criteria

Once hypotheses are narrowed, the clinician applies DSM-5 or ICD-11 criteria meticulously.
Each disorder requires **specific symptom counts, duration, and impairment** levels.

Example:
For **Major Depressive Disorder (MDD)**:

- ≥5 symptoms during the same 2-week period
- Must include depressed mood or anhedonia
- Significant distress or impairment

Pro Tip:
Use **DSM-5-TR symptom checklists** or structured interviews (SCID, MINI).
These tools improve accuracy and reduce "label drift," a common issue where clinicians stretch criteria to fit clients.

Hidden Pitfall:
"Criterion creep"—pathologizing normal sadness or worry.

Remember, DSM disorders require *clinically significant* distress or impairment.

Interesting Angle:
Research shows that using structured diagnostic tools increases accuracy from **60% to 82%**, especially for mood and anxiety disorders (First et al., 2015).

Step 8: Identify Comorbidities

Comorbidity is the rule, not the exception.
Over **50% of clients with one mental disorder meet criteria for at least one additional diagnosis** (Kessler et al., 2018).

Common patterns:

- Depression + Anxiety (40%)
- PTSD + Substance Use (30%)
- ADHD + Conduct Disorder (25%)
- Borderline Personality + Mood Disorders (50%)

Pro Tip:
Prioritize diagnoses by **severity and treatability**. Address life-threatening or destabilizing disorders first (e.g., substance use, suicidality) before secondary conditions.

Hidden Pitfall:
"Diagnostic stacking"—assigning multiple overlapping labels unnecessarily.
For instance, GAD, Panic Disorder, and Adjustment Disorder may reflect one underlying anxiety spectrum.

Interesting Angle:
The DSM-5 task force noted that comorbidity rates are so high that future models may replace categorical

diagnosis with **dimensional profiles**—a shift already piloted in ICD-11.

9. Integrating Data into a Case Conceptualization

After diagnosis, the counselor synthesizes all findings into a **case conceptualization**—a coherent narrative explaining *why* the client is experiencing current symptoms and *what maintains them*.

A strong conceptualization includes:

1. **Summary of presenting issues**
2. **Predisposing, precipitating, perpetuating, and protective factors** (4 Ps)
3. **Cultural and developmental context**
4. **Diagnostic formulation (DSM/ICD)**
5. **Treatment implications and goals**

Example Case Conceptualization:

Client: 32-year-old female presenting with insomnia, hypervigilance, intrusive memories, and irritability.
Predisposing: Childhood trauma, limited social support.
Precipitating: Recent car accident.
Perpetuating: Avoidance behaviors, negative cognitions.
Protective: Stable employment, spiritual faith.
Diagnosis: PTSD, moderate.
Treatment Focus: Trauma-focused CBT, gradual exposure, relaxation training.

Pro Tip:
Write conceptualizations as if for a **multidisciplinary team**—concise, evidence-based, jargon-free.

Clarity fosters collaboration.

Hidden Pitfall:
Treating conceptualizations as static.
They should evolve as new data emerges.
Revisit and update at least every **6–8 sessions**.

10. Quantitative and Qualitative Data Integration

Strong clinical reasoning involves blending **numbers and narratives**:

Quantitative Data	Qualitative Data
Standardized test scores (e.g., BDI-II = 29, moderate depression)	Client narratives ("I feel hopeless every morning.")
Frequency counts (panic attacks = 3/week)	Descriptive tone, metaphors, themes
MSE observations	Family history, cultural meaning of symptoms

Interesting Angle:
Combining quantitative and qualitative data produces **diagnostic accuracy above 85%**, compared to 63% for either alone (Groth-Marnat & Wright, 2016).

? **Pro Tip:**
When data conflicts (e.g., high anxiety score but calm presentation), **note the discrepancy explicitly.** These inconsistencies often reveal deeper psychological defenses or response biases.

11. Common Diagnostic Pitfalls

Pitfall	Description	Correction
Anchoring Bias	Settling on the first plausible diagnosis	Delay closure, generate alternatives
Confirmation Bias	Seeking evidence that supports preconceptions	Ask disconfirming questions
Attribution Error	Overemphasizing personality over situation	Explore environmental triggers
Overpathologizing	Labeling normal reactions as disorders	Evaluate impairment level
Cultural Blindness	Ignoring cultural expressions of distress	Use DSM-5 Cultural Formulation Interview

Interesting Angle:
Even AI diagnostic models exhibit human-like biases when trained on clinician data, proving that **bias is systemic, not personal** (Grote et al., 2020).
Awareness is the first antidote.

12. Ethical Considerations in Diagnosis

Diagnosis carries ethical weight—it affects treatment access, stigma, and self-concept.
Clinicians must balance accuracy with empathy and respect for client autonomy.

- Obtain **informed consent** before diagnostic labeling.
- Discuss the purpose of diagnosis ("to guide care," not "to define you").
- Use **non-stigmatizing language** ("a person experiencing psychosis," not "a psychotic").
- Protect diagnostic information under HIPAA and ethical

confidentiality standards.

Pro Tip:
When in doubt, use a **working diagnosis** (e.g., "Depressive Disorder, Unspecified") until sufficient data emerges.
This preserves accuracy and flexibility.

Hidden Pitfall:
Over-reliance on insurance-driven coding.
Don't let reimbursement criteria distort clinical reality.

Interesting Angle:
Surveys show that **78% of clients** view diagnosis more positively when counselors frame it as *"a roadmap for healing"* rather than *"a label for illness."*

13. The Role of Supervision and Consultation

Consultation is an ethical and professional safeguard in complex diagnostic situations.

- Use **peer consultation** to challenge assumptions.
- Seek supervision for cases involving suicidality, psychosis, or legal risk.
- Document all supervisory guidance in the clinical record.

Pro Tip:
Maintain a **diagnostic decision log**—a brief note documenting your reasoning.
This protects you legally and strengthens clinical growth over time.

Hidden Pitfall:
Avoid "diagnostic isolation."
Counselors working alone are twice as likely to

commit diagnostic oversights compared to those in collaborative teams (Nelson et al., 2019).

14. Summary and Integration

Differential diagnosis and case conceptualization represent the counselor's **most intellectually demanding task**—a synthesis of art, science, and ethics.

Key takeaways:

- Always test, refine, and challenge hypotheses.
- Integrate both scientific rigor and human empathy.
- Update conceptualizations as new evidence emerges.
- Use supervision and structured tools to maintain objectivity.

When done well, the diagnostic process not only clarifies "what's wrong" but also illuminates **what's possible**—offering clients a roadmap to recovery, growth, and restored self-understanding.

Final Interesting Angle:
Diagnostic accuracy improves not just with knowledge, but with *reflective practice.* Counselors who review and critique their own diagnostic decisions show **40% greater improvement** in clinical outcomes (Hill & Lent, 2020).

```
+------------------+   +----------------+   +---------------------+
| ASSESSMENT      |   | DIAGNOSIS    |   | CASE                |
| DATA        |-->|  (The 'What') |-->| CONCEPTUALIZATION
|
| (The 'Raw Info')|   |              |   | (The 'Why')         |
+------------------+   +----------------+   +---------------------+
| - Interview data |   | - F41.1 GAD   |   | Precipitants: Job   |
| - MSE observations|  | - R/O MDD     |   |  loss, financial str.|
| - PHQ-9, GAD-7   |   |               |   | Predisposing: Family |
| - Strengths:     |   |               |   |  history of anxiety |
|  social support  |   |               |   | Perpetuating:       |
+------------------+   +----------------+   |  Avoidance, negative |
                                          |  self-talk          |
                                          | Protective Factors:  |
                                          |  Strong social support|
                                          +---------------------+
                                                 |
                                                 v
                                           +---------------------+
                                           |  TREAMENT PLAN      |
                                           |  (The 'How')        |
                                           +---------------------+
                                           | - CBT for worry     |
                                           | - Exposure therapy  |
                                           | - Social support    |
                                           |  mobilization       |
                                           +---------------------+
```

This diagram shows how assessment data and diagnosis combine to form a comprehensive case conceptualization, which directly informs the treatment plan.

Chapter 3: Populations and Clinical Presentations

Part I: Overview of Common Disorders

1. Introduction: Mapping the Landscape of Psychopathology

Clinical counselors must navigate a complex landscape of mental health disorders that differ in **prevalence, severity, etiology, and treatment response**. The ability to **identify patterns across populations**—while avoiding overgeneralization—is central to clinical excellence.

? **Data Highlight:**
According to the *National Institute of Mental Health (NIMH, 2024)*, approximately **21% of adults in the U.S.** experience a mental illness in a given year—translating to roughly **57.8 million individuals**. Among these, **anxiety disorders** account for **19.1%**, **mood disorders** for **8.4%**, and **personality disorders** for about **9.1%** of the adult population.

? *Insight:*
Understanding disorders as **dimensional** rather than **categorical** —that is, existing on a continuum of severity—enhances clinical accuracy and reduces stigma. Most people who meet criteria for one disorder meet criteria for at least one more, underscoring the complexity of comorbidity.

2. Anxiety Disorders: The Most Prevalent Clinical Group

Anxiety disorders are the **most common** category of psychiatric conditions, affecting approximately **301 million people worldwide (WHO, 2023)**. They represent both **evolutionary adaptive mechanisms** (alertness and threat detection) and **pathological dysfunctions** when the response becomes disproportionate or persistent.

2.1 Core Anxiety Presentations

- **Generalized Anxiety Disorder (GAD)** – Characterized by excessive, uncontrollable worry lasting ≥6 months about various life domains.
- **Panic Disorder** – Recurrent, unexpected panic attacks followed by persistent concern or maladaptive behavioral changes.
- **Social Anxiety Disorder (SAD)** – Fear of social scrutiny or negative evaluation.
- **Specific Phobia** – Marked fear or avoidance of specific stimuli (heights, animals, needles, etc.).
- **Agoraphobia** – Fear of being in situations where escape may be difficult.

Epidemiological Note:
Lifetime prevalence rates show **GAD (5.7%)**, **SAD (7.1%)**, **Panic Disorder (4.7%)**, and **Specific Phobia (9.1%)** (Kessler et al., 2019).

Pro-Tip:
During intake, counselors should **differentiate GAD from Adjustment Disorder with Anxiety**. If the anxiety symptoms have a clear, time-limited stressor, and duration <6 months, the latter may be more appropriate.

Hidden Pitfall:
Clinicians frequently **overestimate the intensity** of anxiety symptoms due to **self-report bias**—clients often describe somatic symptoms (heart racing, chest pain) that mimic medical conditions such as hyperthyroidism or cardiac arrhythmia. Always rule out medical causes before confirming a psychological diagnosis.

Disorder	COGNITIVE (Thoughts)	PHYSICAL (Body Feelings)	BEHAVIORAL (Actions)	KEY FOCUS OF FEAR
Generalized Anxiety Disorder (GAD)	Excessive, uncontrollable worry about various topics	Restlessness, muscle tension, fatigue, sleep disturbance	Procrastination, seeking reassurance, difficulty concentrating	Everyday life & "what if..."
Panic Disorder	Fear of dying, losing control, or "going crazy"	Palpitations, sweating, trembling, chest pain, nausea, chills	Agitation, fleeing, seeking medical help, avoiding exercise/caffeine	The sensations of panic itself
Social Anxiety Disorder (SAD)	Fear of being judged, embarrassed, or humiliated	Blushing, sweating, trembling, mind going blank, nausea	Avoidance of social situations, speaking quietly, avoiding eye contact	Negative evaluation in social situations

| Specific Phobia | Immediate, | Panic-like symptoms | Active avoidance or | A specific object |

| | irrational fear of | (e.g., heart racing) | endurance with intense | or situation |

| | the object/situation| when confronted with it | anxiety | |

+---------------------+--------------------+------------------------
+------------------------+------------------+

| Agoraphobia | Fear that escape | Panic-like symptoms | Avoidance of public | Being in places |

| | might be difficult | when in "unsafe" places | transportation, open | where escape is |

| | or help unavailable | | spaces, crowds, or | hard |

| | if panic-like symptoms occur | | being outside alone | |

+---------------------+--------------------+------------------------
+------------------------+------------------+

This table compares how core anxiety symptoms manifest across different disorders.

3. Mood Disorders: The Spectrum of Affective Dysregulation

Mood disorders encompass **Major Depressive Disorder (MDD)**, **Persistent Depressive Disorder (Dysthymia)**, **Bipolar I Disorder**, and **Bipolar II Disorder**. These represent disturbances in mood regulation—ranging from depressive lows to manic highs.

3.1 Major Depressive Disorder (MDD)

Defined by the presence of ≥5 symptoms (e.g., depressed mood, anhedonia, sleep disturbance, fatigue, guilt, concentration issues, suicidal ideation) over a 2-week period.

Data Highlight:

Globally, MDD affects **~280 million people** (WHO, 2024). In the U.S., **8.3% of adults** had at least one major depressive episode in the past year. Women are nearly **twice as likely** to experience MDD as men.

Insight:
Cognitive theorists (Beck, 1979) emphasize the **cognitive triad** —negative views of self, world, and future—as central to depressive schemas.

Common Misconception:
Many new clinicians assume MDD always involves overt sadness. However, **anhedonia and irritability**—especially in men and adolescents—are often **primary** indicators.

Pro-Tip:
Use **Patient Health Questionnaire-9 (PHQ-9)** routinely. Scores ≥10 suggest moderate depression, while ≥20 indicate severe depression requiring prompt intervention or psychiatric referral.

3.2 Bipolar Disorders

Bipolar disorders are marked by oscillation between **depressive** and **manic/hypomanic** states.

- **Bipolar I**: At least one manic episode (lasting ≥1 week).
- **Bipolar II**: Hypomanic episode (≥4 days) with at least one major depressive episode.

Prevalence:
Bipolar I affects about **1%** and Bipolar II about **1.1%** of adults globally.
The mean age of onset is **25 years**, but subclinical symptoms often appear in late adolescence.

? *Pro-Tip:*
During intake, always screen for **past manic symptoms**, even if the client presents solely with depression. Many "treatment-resistant depressions" are undiagnosed Bipolar II cases.

? *Hidden Pitfall:*
Prescribing antidepressants without mood stabilizers in bipolar clients can **trigger mania or rapid cycling**. Clinical counselors must collaborate closely with prescribing psychiatrists.

4. Trauma-Related Disorders

Trauma is not merely an event but a **psychophysiological process** that overwhelms coping mechanisms. Disorders in this cluster include **Post-Traumatic Stress Disorder (PTSD)**, **Acute Stress Disorder (ASD)**, and **Adjustment Disorders**.

4.1 Post-Traumatic Stress Disorder (PTSD)

PTSD arises following exposure to actual or threatened death, serious injury, or sexual violence—directly, as a witness, or through vicarious means.

Symptoms fall into four clusters:

1. Intrusive memories and flashbacks
2. Avoidance behaviors
3. Negative alterations in cognition and mood
4. Hyperarousal and reactivity

? *Data Highlight:*
Lifetime prevalence: **6.8% in adults** (Kessler et al., 2019). Among veterans, prevalence may exceed **23%**.

? *Interesting Angle:*
Research (van der Kolk, 2014) emphasizes that trauma is **stored somatically**, not only cognitively. Somatic therapies and EMDR have shown **30–45% faster symptom reduction** than talk therapy alone.

? *Pro-Tip:*
Use trauma-informed language during sessions—avoid "What's wrong with you?" and instead use "What happened to you?"

This reduces shame and increases disclosure.

Hidden Pitfall:
Clinicians sometimes mistake **Complex PTSD (C-PTSD)** for Borderline Personality Disorder due to overlapping symptoms (affect dysregulation, identity disturbance). Always assess **trauma history duration and context**.

```
+-----------------------------------+
|    TRIGGER                 |
| (Internal or External)        |
| e.g., Thought, sensation, event  |
+-----------------+----------------+
                  |
                  v
+-----------------------------------+
|   AUTOMATIC NEGATIVE THOUGHT    |
| ("What if...?" Catastrophizing)  |
| e.g., "I'm having a heart attack!"|
|      "I'm going to embarrass myself." |
+-----------------+----------------+
                  |
                  v
+---------------------+---------------------+
|     PHYSICAL SENSATIONS              |
| (Fight-or-Flight Response)            |
|+---------------------+-------------------+ |
|| - Racing Heart     | - Shortness of   | |
|| - Sweating         |  Breath         | |
|| - Trembling        | - Dizziness      | |
|| - Nausea           | - Chest Pain     | |
```

```
|+---------------------+-------------------+ |
+--------------------+----------------------+
                     |
                     v
      +----------------------------------+
|    SAFETY BEHAVIOR / AVOIDANCE    |
| (Immediate Relief but Maintains Cycle) |
| e.g., Leave situation, avoid, seek reassurance |
      +----------------+----------------+
                     |
                     v
      +----------------------------------+
|    NEGATIVE REINFORCEMENT        |
| ("Avoiding worked, the threat is gone.") |
| Beliefs are strengthened, not challenged.|
      +----------------------------------+
```

This diagram illustrates how thoughts, physical feelings, and behaviors interact to maintain and worsen anxiety.

5. Personality Disorders: Enduring Patterns of Interpersonal Dysfunction

Personality disorders (PDs) are enduring patterns of inner experience and behavior that deviate markedly from cultural expectations, are pervasive, inflexible, and lead to distress or impairment.

5.1 DSM-5 Clusters Overview

Cluster	Description	Examples
A	Odd/Eccentric	Paranoid, Schizoid, Schizotypal
B	Dramatic/Errat	Borderline, Narcissistic, Antisocial,

Cluster	Description	Examples
	ic	Histrionic
C	Anxious/Fearful	Avoidant, Dependent, Obsessive-Compulsive

***Prevalence Data*:**
Estimated **9.1%** of U.S. adults meet criteria for at least one PD. **Borderline PD (1.6–5.9%)** and **Antisocial PD (1–4%)** are the most frequently diagnosed in clinical populations.

Insight:
The DSM-5-TR introduces **Alternative Model for Personality Disorders (AMPD)**, focusing on **dimensional traits** (e.g., Negative Affectivity, Detachment, Antagonism, Disinhibition, Psychoticism). This model aligns better with empirical findings and reduces diagnostic overlap.

Pro-Tip:
For Borderline PD, use **Dialectical Behavior Therapy (DBT)**—it has demonstrated **50–60% reduction in self-harm behaviors** after one year (Linehan et al., 2015).

Hidden Pitfall:
Clinicians may inadvertently **reinforce maladaptive attachment** by over-involvement or inconsistent boundaries. Maintain professional detachment while validating the client's emotional experience.

6. Comorbidity and Diagnostic Overlap

Nearly **50% of individuals** who meet diagnostic criteria for one mental disorder meet criteria for at least one other.
Common overlaps:

- Anxiety + Depression (approx. **60% comorbidity**)
- PTSD + Substance Use Disorder (**46%**)
- Personality Disorders + Mood Disorders (**40%**)

Clinical Data:

Comorbidity leads to:

- Longer treatment durations (↑30–50%)
- Higher relapse rates (↑40%)
- Increased hospitalization risk (↑25%)

Interesting Angle:
Comorbidity is often *synergistic* rather than additive. For example, depression amplifies anxiety's physiological arousal, while anxiety worsens depressive rumination.

Pitfall:
Clinicians sometimes focus on the **most visible symptom cluster**, missing underlying primary disorders (e.g., substance use masking PTSD).

Pro-Tip:
Adopt a **hierarchical diagnostic model**:

1. Rule out medical conditions/substances
2. Identify primary vs. secondary disorders
3. Map inter-relational dynamics between conditions

7. Summary of Part I

This overview establishes a foundation for recognizing and conceptualizing the **major categories of clinical presentations** that counselors encounter daily. A diagnostic label is not an endpoint—it is a **starting framework** for individualized, evidence-based treatment.

Key takeaways:

- Anxiety disorders are **most prevalent**, mood disorders are **most disabling**, and trauma-related disorders are **most complex** in etiology.
- Comorbidity is the **rule**, not the exception.
- Personality pathology demands both **boundary clarity**

and **long-term intervention frameworks**.

- Clinicians must **synthesize categorical knowledge (DSM/ICD)** with **dimensional understanding** and **cultural awareness**.

II – Lifespan Considerations: Children, Adolescents, Adults, and Older Adults

1. Introduction: The Lifespan Perspective in Clinical Counseling

The clinical counselor's role extends beyond diagnosing isolated symptoms—it involves understanding **how psychological phenomena evolve and manifest differently** across developmental stages. From attachment disruptions in infancy to cognitive decline in old age, the **expression, impact, and treatment of mental health disorders** are profoundly shaped by **biological maturation, social context, and life transitions**.

Data Highlight:
According to the **World Health Organization (2023)**, mental health disorders account for **16% of the global burden of disease among 10–19-year-olds** and nearly **10% among adults aged 60+**. Yet, fewer than **25%** of these individuals receive appropriate psychological care.

Insight:
Symptoms that appear pathological in one developmental phase may be **normative or adaptive** in another. For instance, separation anxiety is typical in toddlers but concerning when persistent beyond age 8.

2. Clinical Considerations for Children

2.1 Developmental Foundations

Children's mental health is intricately tied to **attachment,**

family dynamics, and neurodevelopment. Cognitive abilities (e.g., abstract thinking, perspective-taking) are still developing, which affects how they perceive and articulate emotional distress.

Data Highlight:

- Approximately **20% of children aged 3–17** in the U.S. have a diagnosable mental disorder (*CDC, 2024*).
- The most common: **ADHD (9.8%)**, **Anxiety Disorders (9.4%)**, and **Behavioral Disorders (8.9%)**.

Interesting Angle:
Early intervention is not only therapeutic—it's **preventative**. Longitudinal data (Moffitt et al., 2018) show that early treatment of conduct and emotional issues reduces adult psychopathology by **30–40%**.

2.2 Common Childhood Disorders

Attention-Deficit/Hyperactivity Disorder (ADHD)

Characterized by inattention, hyperactivity, and impulsivity across settings for ≥6 months.

Pro-Tip:
Always assess both **home and school** environments. Teachers' behavioral checklists (e.g., Conners-4, Vanderbilt) improve diagnostic reliability by **over 25%**.

Pitfall:
Clinicians often **overpathologize normal energy levels** in young boys. True ADHD requires **functional impairment**, not merely high activity.

Autism Spectrum Disorder (ASD)

Marked by deficits in social communication and restricted, repetitive behaviors.

Data Highlight:
Prevalence estimates (CDC, 2024) show **1 in 36** U.S. children diagnosed with ASD, a tenfold increase since the 1990s—partly due to broader criteria and better detection.

Insight:
ASD is not a single entity but a **spectrum**. Each child's cognitive profile, language ability, and sensory processing vary widely.

Pro-Tip:
Combine **developmental history**, **standardized tools** (e.g., ADOS-2, CARS-2), and **clinical observation** for a valid assessment.

Hidden Pitfall:
Parents may **mask symptoms** unintentionally by over-structuring routines at home. Always evaluate the child's adaptability in **novel social contexts**.

Anxiety and Mood Disorders in Children

Children may not express sadness or fear verbally; instead, symptoms manifest somatically (e.g., stomachaches, irritability, school refusal).

Interesting Angle:
Research (Essau et al., 2019) indicates that children's anxiety often **precedes** mood disorders in adolescence—early anxiety is a **predictive marker** of later depression.

Pro-Tip:
Use **play therapy** or **expressive modalities** (art, storytelling) for younger clients to externalize internal states safely.

3. Adolescents: Navigating Identity and Autonomy

Adolescence is marked by **neurobiological remodeling** (prefrontal cortex maturation, dopamine regulation) and **social**

reorientation toward peers. Mental health issues often **first emerge** during this phase.

Data Highlight:

- **1 in 5 adolescents** experience a diagnosable mental health disorder (NIMH, 2024).
- Suicide is the **second leading cause of death** among ages 15–24 globally.
- Peak onset age: **15–25** for mood, anxiety, and psychotic disorders.

Insight:
The adolescent brain is **hypersensitive to reward** and **less responsive to risk**, explaining impulsivity and emotional extremes.

3.1 Common Adolescent Presentations

Depressive Disorders

Adolescents exhibit **irritability, academic decline, and social withdrawal** rather than overt sadness.

Common Pitfall:
Many adults misinterpret irritability as **defiance** rather than a depressive symptom. This misreading delays intervention.

Pro-Tip:
Use screening tools like the **PHQ-A (Adolescent Version)**. Always assess for **suicidal ideation**, even if it seems "out of character."

Substance Use Disorders (SUD)

Adolescents experiment to assert independence or self-medicate emotional pain.

Data Highlight:

By age 18, **55%** of U.S. adolescents have tried alcohol and **17%** have used an illicit drug (Monitoring the Future, 2023).

Interesting Angle:
Substance use is often **developmentally linked** to peer influence and perceived invincibility, rather than pure addiction. Prevention must be **social-contextual**, not just individual.

Pro-Tip:
Use **Motivational Interviewing (MI)**—it's been shown to reduce substance use by **20–30%** compared to punitive or confrontational approaches.

Eating Disorders (EDs)

Anorexia Nervosa, Bulimia Nervosa, and Binge Eating Disorder typically **emerge in adolescence**, with the highest risk in females aged 15–19.

Data Highlight:
Global prevalence: **Anorexia (0.3%), Bulimia (1%), BED (1.9%)** (Treasure et al., 2022). Mortality rate for Anorexia = **5–6%**, one of the highest among psychiatric disorders.

Hidden Pitfall:
Many cases go undiagnosed because patients maintain "normal" BMI (Atypical Anorexia). Always assess **body image distortion and compulsive behaviors**, not just weight metrics.

3.2 Developmental Considerations

- **Identity Formation:** Erikson's stage of *Identity vs. Role Confusion* is central; failure leads to chronic instability and susceptibility to peer pressure.
- **Cognitive Maturity:** Abstract reasoning allows existential questioning—"Who am I?" "What's my purpose?"—which can amplify anxiety or depression.
- **Risk Factors:** Family conflict, academic pressure, social

media exposure, and trauma increase vulnerability.

Pro-Tip:
Involve families as **support systems** rather than **monitors**. Adolescents respond better to **collaborative alliances** than authoritarian structures.

4. Adults: Balancing Autonomy, Responsibility, and Stress

Adult psychopathology often emerges from **role strain**, **relationship breakdown**, and **occupational pressures** rather than pure developmental deficits. Adults must juggle **career identity**, **family roles**, and **self-concept integration**.

Data Highlight:

- Nearly **1 in 5 adults** in the U.S. report a mental illness annually (NIMH, 2024).
- **Depression and anxiety** are the most prevalent, followed by **substance-related disorders**.
- Average onset age for **major depressive episodes**: 32 years.

4.1 Common Adult Presentations

Anxiety and Burnout

Adults often experience **chronic stress**, leading to generalized anxiety, insomnia, and occupational burnout.

Interesting Angle:
Burnout is **not a DSM disorder**, yet it meets many criteria for an adjustment disorder. The WHO (2022) classifies it as an "occupational phenomenon" with distinct physiological markers (elevated cortisol, immune dysregulation).

Pro-Tip:
Cognitive-behavioral stress management (CBSM) and

mindfulness reduce burnout symptoms by **25–40%** over 8–10 weeks (Grossman et al., 2021).

Relationship and Family Disorders

Marital dissatisfaction, domestic violence, and codependency are frequent issues.

Pitfall:
New clinicians often **triangulate unintentionally**, aligning with one partner over another. Remain neutral, focusing on systemic dynamics, not individual blame.

Pro-Tip:
Use **Emotionally Focused Therapy (EFT)** for couples—it demonstrates **70–75% recovery rates** in clinical trials (Johnson, 2020).

Substance Use and Behavioral Addictions

Alcohol, prescription medication, and behavioral addictions (gaming, gambling, pornography) are rising among working adults.

? *Data Highlight:*
In the U.S., **14.5 million adults** have Alcohol Use Disorder (AUD). Behavioral addictions affect **8–12%** of adults globally.

Insight:
Addictions often function as **emotion regulation strategies**—temporary relief mechanisms masking underlying anxiety, trauma, or depression.

5. Older Adults: The Psychology of Aging and Loss

The geriatric population presents **unique diagnostic challenges**—somatic complaints, cognitive decline, and underreporting of psychological symptoms due to stigma or generational attitudes.

Data Highlight:

- Around **15% of adults aged 60+** experience a mental disorder (WHO, 2023).
- **Depression (7%)**, **Dementia (5%)**, and **Anxiety (3.8%)** are the most common.
- Suicide rates are highest in **men aged 75+**, especially those recently widowed or physically ill.

5.1 Common Late-Life Disorders

Depression in Older Adults

Often presents as **fatigue, sleep disturbance, or somatic pain** rather than overt sadness.

Pitfall:
Clinicians frequently attribute symptoms to "normal aging," missing treatable depression.
Use **Geriatric Depression Scale (GDS)** to screen effectively.

Pro-Tip:
Combine **behavioral activation** with **social reconnection** strategies (community involvement, volunteerism). Studies show **25–35% symptom reduction** within 12 weeks.

Dementia and Mild Cognitive Impairment (MCI)

Cognitive decline affects memory, reasoning, and executive functioning. Alzheimer's disease represents **60–70%** of dementia cases.

Data Highlight:
By 2050, global dementia cases are projected to **triple to 150 million** (Alzheimer's Association, 2024).

Insight:
Cognitive decline often coexists with depression ("pseudodementia"). Treating depression first can restore cognitive performance in up to **40%** of cases.

Grief and Adjustment Disorders

Loss and bereavement are normative but may develop into prolonged grief disorder (DSM-5-TR).

Pro-Tip:
Encourage **life review therapy**—structured reminiscence that helps older adults integrate life meaning and reduce regret.

6. Integrative Developmental Perspective

Every life stage carries distinct vulnerabilities and protective factors:

Stage	Core Tasks	Primary Risks	Protective Factors
Childhood	Attachment, emotional regulation	Neglect, developmental delays	Stable caregivers
Adolescence	Identity, autonomy	Peer pressure, self-harm	Supportive peer & family
Adulthood	Role integration, intimacy	Burnout, addiction	Work-life balance
Older Adulthood	Integrity, acceptance	Isolation, grief	Social connection, meaning

Insight:
Mental health across the lifespan follows a **U-shaped curve**—well-being tends to dip in midlife and rebound in later years, provided physical health and social ties remain intact (Stone et al., 2021).

7. Summary of Part II

Clinical practice requires **developmental sensitivity**—the recognition that psychological symptoms, coping styles, and

therapeutic responsiveness shift across life stages.
Effective counselors tailor **assessment tools, interventions, and communication** to developmental capacity and context.

Key Takeaways:

- **Children:** Focus on play, family systems, and developmental milestones.
- **Adolescents:** Address identity, peer dynamics, and impulsivity.
- **Adults:** Target stress, role strain, and relational adjustment.
- **Older Adults:** Prioritize dignity, cognitive health, and life meaning.

III – Working with Multicultural and Diverse Populations

1. Introduction: Why Multicultural Competence Defines Modern Counseling

In the twenty-first century, clinical practice cannot be separated from the cultural identities and social contexts of the people it serves. The **American Counseling Association (ACA)** and **American Psychological Association (APA)** both assert that multicultural competence is not optional — it is an **ethical imperative** (ACA Code of Ethics, 2014; APA, 2017).

Clients' experiences of **race, ethnicity, gender, religion, socioeconomic status, sexual orientation, age, ability, and migration history** shape the meaning they assign to symptoms, coping styles, and healing practices.

? **Data Highlight:**
According to the U.S. Census Bureau (2024), **over 42% of Americans identify as part of a racial or ethnic minority group**, and **23% of counseling clients** report having a first

language other than English. Globally, cross-border migration has reached **281 million people (UN, 2023)** — an unprecedented cultural intersection in mental health contexts.

Insight:
Cultural diversity doesn't just change *who* seeks counseling; it reshapes *how* distress manifests and *what* "well-being" means in different cultural frameworks.

2. Cultural Competence and Cultural Humility

Cultural competence involves **awareness, knowledge, and skill** (Sue et al., 1992).
However, modern frameworks emphasize **cultural humility** — a lifelong process of self-reflection rather than a static skill set (Hook et al., 2013).

2.1 Awareness: Self as Cultural Being

Effective clinicians recognize that **their own worldview is culturally constructed**.
This involves examining implicit biases, privilege, and ethnocentric assumptions that may unconsciously influence assessment and treatment.

> ***Pitfall:***
> A counselor assumes "assertiveness" indicates mental health progress in a collectivist client, overlooking that harmony and humility may be culturally valued more than verbal self-expression.

2.2 Knowledge: Understanding Cultural Contexts

Clinicians need to grasp how **history, colonization, systemic oppression, and acculturation** shape clients' experiences.
For instance, indigenous clients may present "symptoms" that are deeply tied to intergenerational trauma and cultural loss —

issues that Western diagnostic models can misinterpret.

? **Data Highlight:**
Studies show that **African American and Latinx clients are 30–40% less likely** to receive appropriate depression treatment compared to white clients (Snowden, 2018).

2.3 Skills: The Multicultural Counseling Toolkit

Practical multicultural competence includes:

- Using **culturally responsive assessment tools**
- Incorporating **client's explanatory model of illness**
- Employing **language services** or bilingual therapy when needed
- Adjusting interventions to **fit cultural communication norms**

Pro-Tip:
When possible, begin each intake with a **"Cultural Formulation Interview"** (from DSM-5-TR Appendix) to understand the client's view of their problem, cause, and healing expectations.

3. Cross-Cultural Diagnostic Validity

Diagnosing across cultures is inherently complex.
Most psychiatric frameworks (like DSM and ICD) were developed based on **Western individualist norms**, which can inadvertently pathologize culturally normative behaviors.

3.1 Cultural Concepts of Distress

DSM-5-TR introduced "**Cultural Concepts of Distress**" (CCD) to account for these variations — encompassing:

- **Cultural syndromes** (e.g., *ataque de nervios*, *kufungisisa*)

- **Cultural idioms of distress** (e.g., "heavy heart," "nervous breakdown")
- **Cultural explanations** (beliefs about causes like spirits or family disharmony)

? **Data Highlight:**
Cross-national research in *The Lancet Psychiatry* (2022) found that **symptom expression varies by over 60%** between collectivist and individualist cultures — particularly in somatic vs. emotional expression.

> ***Insight:***
> A Cambodian refugee describing "burning in the chest" may be expressing depression through a culturally shaped somatic idiom rather than a purely medical symptom.

3.2 Differential Diagnosis Across Cultures

Clinicians must disentangle whether a presentation is:

- **Culturally normative**,
- **A stress response**, or
- **Indicative of pathology**.

> *Pitfall:*
> Mistaking culturally sanctioned spirit possession or trance states for psychosis can lead to unnecessary medication and stigma.

3.3 Using Cultural Formulation in Practice

The DSM's **Cultural Formulation Interview (CFI)** includes 16 questions addressing:

- Client's view of their problem
- Cultural identity and supports

- Cultural stressors
- Cultural features of the clinician-client relationship

Pro-Tip:
Integrate the CFI early — it increases diagnostic accuracy by up to **25% (Lewis-Fernández et al., 2017)** and strengthens therapeutic alliance.

4. Systemic and Structural Barriers to Care

Even the most culturally competent clinician operates within **systems** — healthcare, insurance, education, and justice — that can either empower or marginalize clients.

4.1 Access and Utilization Disparities

- **Language barriers** prevent over **12% of immigrant clients** from accessing consistent therapy.
- **Financial constraints**: Uninsured populations are **2.8 times less likely** to complete treatment.
- **Rural and indigenous communities** face provider shortages, with ratios as high as **1 counselor per 10,000 residents** (APA, 2022).

  Pitfall:
  Focusing on individual "motivation" or "resistance" without considering systemic barriers reinforces inequity.

4.2 Implicit Bias and Diagnostic Injustice

Research reveals implicit racial bias impacts diagnosis and treatment:

- African American men are **3–5 times more likely** to be diagnosed with schizophrenia when presenting similar symptoms to white counterparts diagnosed with bipolar disorder (Whaley, 2019).

- LGBTQ+ youth often experience **diagnostic overshadowing**, where their identity is incorrectly assumed to "cause" mental illness rather than co-exist with it.

Insight:
"Cultural blindness" — treating all clients "the same" — is not equality; it's **erasure of difference**.

4.3 Intersectionality: The Overlapping Systems of Identity

Coined by Kimberlé Crenshaw (1989), **intersectionality** examines how identities like race, gender, and class intersect to create unique experiences of oppression or privilege. Counselors must view clients holistically — for example, understanding that a Black transgender woman may face compounded stigma affecting mental health.

Pro-Tip:
Use an **"intersectional case formulation"** to map the client's social ecology — micro (individual), meso (community), and macro (institutional) influences.

5. Evidence-Based Multicultural Interventions

Integrating cultural responsiveness into interventions is not about abandoning evidence-based models — it's about **adapting them**.

5.1 Cultural Adaptation of Evidence-Based Treatments

Bernal et al. (2009) identified eight elements of cultural adaptation:

1. Language
2. Persons (therapist-client match)

3. Metaphors
4. Content
5. Concepts
6. Goals
7. Methods
8. Context

Data Highlight:
Meta-analyses show **culturally adapted interventions** have **70% higher retention** and **50% better symptom improvement** compared to non-adapted ones (Griner & Smith, 2006; Chow et al., 2021).

5.2 Multicultural Techniques Across Modalities

- **CBT:** Incorporate culturally relevant metaphors; adjust cognitive restructuring to honor collective values.
- **Family Systems Therapy:** Emphasize cultural hierarchies and filial piety.
- **Mindfulness Approaches:** Acknowledge non-Western roots (e.g., Buddhist origins) to prevent cultural appropriation.

Pro-Tip:
Ask clients: "How do people in your culture usually deal with stress or sadness?" Their answer provides culturally congruent entry points for intervention.

6. Supervision, Training, and the Counselor's Cultural Growth

Cultural competence is developmental, not declarative.

6.1 The Multicultural Counseling Competence Continuum

1. **Cultural destructiveness**
2. **Cultural incapacity**
3. **Cultural blindness**
4. **Cultural pre-competence**
5. **Cultural competence**
6. **Cultural proficiency**

Pitfall:
Believing one's "diversity training" is ever complete — cultural contexts evolve as rapidly as global demographics.

6.2 Culturally Responsive Supervision

Supervisors should model openness, encourage discussion of racial identity dynamics, and address microaggressions in supervision.
Structured reflection tools like **the Multicultural Supervision Competence Scale (MSCS)** (Inman et al., 2018) help track growth.

Insight:
Culturally attuned supervision decreases counselor burnout by fostering authenticity and empathy (Owen et al., 2019).

7. Clinical Case Example: Intersectional Practice in Action

Case Summary:
"Fatima," a 32-year-old Muslim woman, immigrated from Morocco to Canada five years ago. She presents with panic attacks and chronic fatigue.
A Western-trained clinician initially suspects *panic disorder with agoraphobia*, but through the Cultural Formulation Interview, Fatima describes symptoms as "losing harmony with God" and physical "tightness in the chest."

Therapeutic Process:
The counselor integrates psychoeducation about anxiety with spiritual coping strategies from Islamic psychology, using Fatima's faith-based framework to enhance agency and meaning.
Over 12 sessions, panic frequency decreases by 65%, and Fatima reports "restored balance."

> ***Pro-Tip:***
> Align evidence-based interventions with clients' spiritual and cultural schemas — this strengthens engagement and outcomes.

8. Summary and Integration

- Cultural humility and competence are **lifelong disciplines**.
- Cross-cultural diagnostic accuracy requires the use of **structured tools** like the CFI.
- **Intersectionality** deepens understanding of clients' layered experiences.
- Systemic advocacy is part of ethical practice.

Final Data Highlight:
Clinicians with formal multicultural training report **40% fewer diagnostic errors** and **60% higher client satisfaction** (APA Multicultural Task Force, 2023).

Closing Insight:
The best multicultural clinicians don't claim expertise in every culture — they commit to **curiosity, humility, and cultural partnership** with every client they meet.

Chapter 4 : Exam-Style Case Scenarios & Question Quiz (with Answers)

All aligned to NCMHCE structure, including DSM-5-TR relevance, ethics, and outcome-based decision making.

=Add-On A — Exam-Style Case Scenarios (EBP + Stats)

These scenarios reflect **how the NCMHCE tests clinical reasoning.Case 1 — Using Outcome Measures to Adjust Treatment**

You're treating a client with Panic Disorder using CBT-Panic. Initial PDSS (Panic Disorder Severity Scale) score: **15 (moderate)**

After 6 sessions:

- PDSS score ↓ to **14**
- Client reports **no reduction** in panic attacks
- Moderate session attendance

Which step follows EBP principles?

A) Continue unchanged
B) Add anti-anxiety medication without assessment
C) Consult with supervisor + modify treatment plan
D) Terminate therapy

✓ **Correct: C**
Minimal statistical + **no clinical improvement → adjust intervention**.

Exam Tip: *When outcomes stall → modify*

Case 2 — Cultural Validity of Measures

Client: 52-year-old immigrant from a culture where emotional disclosure is stigmatized. PHQ-9 score: **5 (mild)** but client reports **severe insomnia and withdrawal**.

Best response?

A) Accept PHQ-9 results as sole baseline
B) Add qualitative interview + cultural formulation
C) Diagnose MDD immediately
D) Replace therapy with medication only

✅ **Correct: B**
Symptoms under-reported → expand culturally sensitive assessment.

Exam Tip: *Scores ≠ full story — always consider culture*

Case 3 — Clinically Meaningful Change

Client in trauma therapy shows:

Time	PCL-5 Score
Baseline	46 (severe)
Session 8	41
Session 16	28

What does this show?

A) Clinically significant progress
B) Worsening PTSD
C) Only statistical improvement
D) No change

✅ **Correct: A**
A **≥10-point drop** on PCL-5 = clinically meaningful improvement.

Memory trick: **"PCL = 10 to tell"**
(10-point drop = *tell* improvement)

Case 4 — Study Design Interpretation

A school social worker tests a depression curriculum in **one classroom** with before/after PHQ-9 data.

This is what research design?

A) Randomized controlled trial
B) Single group pre-post study
C) Case-control trial
D) Meta-analysis

✅ **Correct: B**

Exam Tip: *One group + no comparison = pre-post*

Case 5 — Reliability Concern

A symptom rating scale gives **wildly different scores** when used by different counselors.

Which type of reliability failed?

A) Internal consistency
B) Test-retest reliability
C) Inter-rater reliability
D) Construct validity

✅ **Correct: C**

? One-liner: **Raters disagree → inter-rater reliability**

✅ *More scenarios available — we can continue to 10, 20, or 50 cases.*

Add-On B — 20-Question Quiz (with Answers)

Select the best answer:
(Answers at the bottom)

1. EBP includes research, clinical expertise, and:
   A) Personal beliefs
   B) Client values + preferences

C) Insurance requirements
D) Supervisor opinions

2. High **standard deviation** means:
A) Scores cluster close together
B) Outcomes differ widely
C) Measurement is invalid
D) Scores are mostly zero

3. Which evidence type is strongest?
A) Expert opinion
B) Meta-analysis
C) Case study
D) One clinician's experience

4. A measure can be **reliable** but not:
A) Valid
B) Administered
C) Consistent
D) Used

5. Test-retest reliability checks:
A) Agreement between raters
B) Stability across time
C) Cultural appropriateness
D) Predicting future behavior

6. Cultural mismatch reduces:
A) Test-retest reliability
B) Validity
C) Random sampling
D) Experimental control

7. Which design best supports **causality**?
A) Systematic review
B) RCT
C) Focus group
D) Case report

8. A **clinically significant** result means:

A) Statistically significant only
B) Meaningful symptom improvement
C) Therapist feels it worked
D) Outcome measure wasn't used

9. Effectiveness studies evaluate:
   A) Controlled research efficacy
   B) Real-world outcomes
   C) Only short-term effects
   D) Marketing strategies

10. PHQ-9 measures:
   A) Panic severity
   B) Substance use
   C) Depression symptoms
   D) Cognitive impairment

11. ACA ethics require counselors use:
   A) Personal preference
   B) Evidence-based approaches
   C) Social media polls
   D) Newest trends

12. GAD-7 is used for:
   A) Sleep disorder
   B) Anxiety
   C) Conduct problems
   D) Autism

13. High **construct validity** means:
   A) Items match intended concept
   B) Two clinicians agree
   C) Test is stable
   D) Test is cheap

14. A survey with open-ended questions is:
   A) Quantitative
   B) Qualitative
   C) Meta-analytic

D) Invalid

15. Program evaluation that examines "Was intervention delivered correctly?" is:
    A) Process evaluation
    B) Outcome evaluation
    C) Experimental control
    D) Benchmarking

16. Outcome measures must be used:
    A) Only at intake
    B) At baseline + throughout + end of treatment
    C) Only if funding requires
    D) Rarely

17. A reduction in PCL-5 score of **2 points** means:
    A) Clinically meaningful improvement
    B) Minimal change
    C) Relapse
    D) Invalid results

18. Inter-rater reliability ensures:
    A) Scores correlate with client report
    B) Therapist judgment doesn't bias scoring
    C) Cost effectiveness
    D) Cultural sensitivity

19. Phenomenology is:
    A) Statistical comparison
    B) Understanding lived experience
    C) Testing medication
    D) Measuring heart rate

20. Systematic review conclusion:
    A) Unreliable
    B) Best available research summary
    C) Only expert opinion
    D) Industry marketing

✅Quiz Answer Key

1-B, 2-B, 3-B, 4-A, 5-B, 6-B, 7-B, 8-B, 9-B, 10-C, 11-B, 12-B, 13-A, 14-B, 15-A, 16-B, 17-B, 18-B, 19-B, 20-B

✅Reliability vs. Validity Table

Concept	Meaning	Key Question	Quick Check
Reliability	Consistency	"Are results stable?"	Cronbach's $\alpha \geq .70$
Validity	Accuracy	"Does this measure what it should?"	Cultural match needed

Mnemonic: **CRAVE**

- **C**onsistency = **R**eliability
- **A**ccuracy = **V**alidity
- **E**vidence supports both

Mnemonic: **"MO ME MEAN SD"**
Mode → Median → Mean → Standard Deviation
(Ordered from simplest to most complex)

✅Clinical Significance Shortcut

PCL = 10 to tell
(10-point decrease = clinically meaningful)

PHQ-9 = 5 to thrive
(5-point decrease = meaningful)

✅Research Method Selection Chart

Best Choice When…	Design
You want causality	RCT
You want symptom change over time in 1 client	Single-case

Best Choice When…	Design
You want lived experience	Qualitative
You want real-world results	Effectiveness study

Chapter 5: Essential Counseling Techniques and Interventions

Mastering Practical Skills for Effective Clinical Practice
(Structured for NCMHCE exam objectives)

Section 5.1 — Core Counseling Skills Across Theories

To perform clinically, you have to know **what intervention fits when** — and WHY.

Theory	Focus	Key Techniques	When to Use	NCMHCE Trigger Words
CBT	Thoughts → Emotions → Behavior	Cognitive restructuring, behavioral activation, exposure, thought logs	Anxiety, depression, OCD, PTSD	Distorted thinking, avoidant behavior, core beliefs
Humanistic	Self-concept & personal growth	Unconditional positive regard, empathy, reflection of feeling	Identity issues, grief, self-esteem	Congruence, unconditional acceptance
Psychodynamic	Unconscious patterns & past conflicts	Interpretation, exploring transference, insight building	Personality disorders, trauma history	Defense mechanisms, unresolved conflicts
Solution-Focused	Strengths + Future goals	Miracle question,	Clinical stabilizat	*What's working?*

Theory	Focus	Key Techniques	When to Use	NCMHCE Trigger Words
Brief Therapy (SFBT)		scaling, exception finding	ion, brief episodes	’ strengths focus
Motivational Interviewing (MI)	Ambivalence toward change	OARS, decisional balance, rolling with resistance	Substance use, lifestyle issues	Change talk, readiness to change
DBT	Emotion regulation & distress tolerance	Chain analysis, mindfulness, STOP, radical acceptance	BPD, suicidality, emotional dysregulation	Self-harm, interpersonal chaos

NCMHCE Pro-Tip:
If the client is **unsafe**, **unable to think logically**, or **in active crisis — NO insight or long-term work** yet. You stabilize first.

Section 5.2 — Crisis Intervention & Suicide Assessment

When safety is in question → **STOP AND ASSESS** ?

Columbia-Suicide Severity Rating Scale (C-SSRS) Essentials

Ask about:
1□ Ideation
2□Intent
3□Plan
4□Means
5□ Past attempts

If **intent + plan + means** = ? **Immediate safety escalation**

✅ Crisis Intervention Algorithm (Memory Mnemonic: SAFETY)

Letter	Action	Example
S	**S**creen for suicide risk	Ask directly: "Are you thinking of killing yourself?"
A	**A**ssess intent, plan, means	Determine lethality
F	**F**ollow safety protocol	Remove access to means, involve supports
E	**E**stablish safety plan	Warning signs, coping tools, contacts
T	**T**herapeutic alliance	Empathy & collaboration
Y	**Y**ield to higher level of care if needed	ER, involuntary hospitalization

Always document rationale for safety decisions → major scoring point on NCMHCE.

Section 5.3 — Techniques for Common Clinical Problems

This is where targeted interventions shine.

Substance Use Disorders (AUD, OUD, SUDs)

Phase	Intervention	Goal
Pre-contemplation	MI	Explore ambivalence, build discrepancy
Early Recovery	CBT, psychoeducation, relapse prevention	Identify triggers & coping skills
Stabilization	Group therapy / MAT	Accountability &

Phase	Intervention	Goal
		neurological support
High relapse risk	Contingency management, DBT distress tolerance	Reinforce sobriety

Avoid shame-based confrontation — pushes withdrawal from treatment.

Grief & Loss (Complicated vs. normative grief)

Healthy Grief	Complicated / Prolonged Grief
Tearfulness, sadness, temporary functional impacts	Persistent functional decline >6 months
Acceptance grows	Denial persists
Some joy returns	Rumination dominates
Supportive therapy helpful	**Refer to grief specialist**

Interventions:
✅Meaning-making
✅Supportive counseling
✅Ritual + remembrance therapy

NCMHCE Tip: DO NOT label normal grief as a disorder unless **functional impairment is severe**.

Anger Dysregulation

CBT + Skills training are first-line

- Cognitive reframing → challenge hostile attribution bias
- Relaxation: diaphragmatic breathing, PMR
- Behavioral rehearsal → assertiveness skills
- Trigger mapping + coping replacement behaviors

? Look for comorbid issues: trauma, substance use, impulse

control

Section 5.4 — Case Examples + Clinical Decisions

✅Case #1: Panic in Public

Client: 27-year-old, recurrent panic in crowds, avoids malls.

BEST FIRST MOVE:
→ Psychoeducation + CBT exposure hierarchy

AVOID:
→ Psychodynamic exploration of childhood (not immediate)

✅Case #2: Substance Use + Court Mandate

Angry 32-year-old male required to attend therapy.

BEST:
→ Motivational Interviewing ("What would change look like for you?")

AVOID:
→ Confrontation → escalates resistance

✅Case #3: Suicidal Teen

15-year-old expresses "I have a plan to take pills."

BEST:
→ Engage parents + remove access + ER referral

NEVER:
→ Promise confidentiality

Quick Mnemonics

Topic	Memory Tool
Suicide assessment	**PLAN-M** — Plan, Lethality, Access, intent Now, Means
CBT thought errors	**FOGGED** — Fortune telling, Overgeneralizing, Global labeling, etc.
MI change talk	**DARN-CAT** — Desire, Ability, Reason, Need → Commitment, Action, Taking steps

Chapter 6: Case Studies and Clinical Scenarios

This chapter presents a series of realistic case studies designed to develop practical counseling skills across diverse client populations. Each scenario highlights key assessment points, counseling interventions, and ethical or cultural issues counselors may encounter in real-world practice.

Use these cases to practice conceptualization, treatment planning, and intervention design. After each scenario, review the analysis and discussion questions to strengthen your applied counseling judgment.

1. Children and Adolescents

Case: "Ethan, the Anxious Fifth Grader"

Background:
Ethan, a 10-year-old boy, was referred by his teacher due to frequent stomachaches, tearfulness before school, and reluctance to participate in group activities. His parents describe him as "bright but shy." Recently, he's been refusing to attend school and expresses fear that "something bad will happen" to his mom while he's gone.

Assessment Focus:

- School avoidance and anxiety symptoms
- Family dynamics and attachment
- Peer relationships and social confidence
- Developmental stage and coping skills

Conceptualization:
Ethan presents with symptoms consistent with **Separation Anxiety Disorder**. His anxiety appears to stem from overprotection at home and difficulty tolerating uncertainty or separation.

Intervention Strategies:

- **Cognitive-Behavioral Play Therapy (CBPT):** Introduce coping tools through games and drawing.
- **Exposure and Desensitization:** Gradual return-to-school plan (e.g., visit classroom → attend half day → full day).
- **Parental Coaching:** Teach parents to reinforce independence and avoid excessive reassurance.
- **School Collaboration:** Partner with teachers to ensure a supportive environment.

Ethical Considerations:

- Obtain parental consent and child assent.
- Maintain confidentiality while coordinating with school staff.
- Use developmentally appropriate language and materials.

Counselor Tip:
Use "feelings thermometers" or "worry meters" to help Ethan externalize anxiety and measure progress visually.

2. Adults

Case: "Maria and the Weight of Burnout"

Background:
Maria, 34, is a nurse working long shifts in a hospital. She reports irritability, insomnia, emotional numbness, and feeling "disconnected" from her patients. Her performance is declining, and she fears disciplinary action.

Assessment Focus:

- Occupational stress and compassion fatigue
- Coping patterns and perfectionism

- Social support and work-life balance
- Rule out major depressive disorder or substance use

Conceptualization:
Maria's symptoms are consistent with **Burnout Syndrome** and secondary traumatic stress. Her high empathy and self-imposed standards have created emotional exhaustion.

Intervention Strategies:

- **Mindfulness-Based Stress Reduction (MBSR):** Teach grounding and breathing exercises before and after shifts.
- **Cognitive Restructuring:** Challenge self-critical thoughts ("I must always be strong").
- **Behavioral Activation:** Encourage restorative activities and reconnecting with supportive peers.
- **Workplace Advocacy:** Discuss boundaries and possible schedule adjustments.

Ethical Considerations:

- Address risk of impaired professional functioning.
- Ensure informed consent if recommending outside support or referrals.
- Monitor for signs of major depression or suicidal ideation.

Counselor Tip:
Encourage micro self-care practices—two-minute deep-breath breaks or gratitude journaling between shifts.

3. Couples and Families

Case: "The Jacksons and the Silent Dinner Table"

Background:
Mark (42) and Alyssa (40) have been married 15 years. They report "living like roommates." Their teenage son, Liam (15),

has become withdrawn and spends hours gaming alone.

Assessment Focus:

- Communication patterns and emotional intimacy
- Family structure and roles
- Parenting alignment and conflict
- Family strengths and motivation for change

Conceptualization:
This family exhibits **disengaged communication** and low emotional attunement. The presenting issue is marital disconnection, but secondary concerns include parenting inconsistency and adolescent avoidance.

Intervention Strategies:

- **Structural Family Therapy:** Clarify roles and strengthen the parental subsystem.
- **Emotionally Focused Couples Therapy (EFT):** Rebuild attachment through vulnerability exercises.
- **Family Activities:** Reinstate weekly shared meals or outdoor activities to increase connection.

Ethical Considerations:

- Obtain consent from all family members; explain limits of confidentiality in family sessions.
- Maintain neutrality and avoid alignment with one partner.
- Assess for potential domestic violence before conjoint sessions.

Counselor Tip:
Use "speaker-listener" exercises at home to rebuild safe communication without interruption or blame.

4. Older Adults and Aging Populations

Case: "Mr. Lee and the Empty Apartment"

Background:
Mr. Lee, 78, recently lost his wife of 52 years. He reports difficulty sleeping, lack of appetite, and feelings of "pointlessness." His adult children live out of state. He spends most days watching TV alone.

Assessment Focus:

- Grief and loss reaction
- Social isolation and physical health
- Cognitive screening (rule out depression-related memory issues)
- Life review and meaning

Conceptualization:
Mr. Lee is experiencing **complicated grief** compounded by social isolation. His symptoms overlap with mild depressive features but remain grief-centered.

Intervention Strategies:

- **Grief Counseling and Reminiscence Therapy:** Facilitate storytelling about his marriage and life meaning.
- **Behavioral Activation:** Encourage re-engagement with community centers or faith groups.
- **Intergenerational Connection:** Video calls or letters with grandchildren to strengthen social ties.

Ethical Considerations:

- Respect autonomy and decision-making capacity.
- Monitor for suicidal thoughts or severe depression.
- Address cultural views of aging and family duty.

Counselor Tip:
Encourage life review projects such as photo scrapbooks or recorded stories — these reinforce legacy and purpose.

5. Multicultural and Diverse Populations

Case: "Nadia Navigates Two Worlds"

Background:
Nadia, 22, is a second-generation Moroccan American college student. She reports stress balancing her family's traditional expectations with her personal goals for independence. Her parents expect her to marry soon, but she wishes to pursue graduate school first.

Assessment Focus:

- Cultural identity and acculturation stress
- Family expectations vs. personal autonomy
- Coping styles and social support
- Intersectional factors (gender, culture, religion)

Conceptualization:
Nadia experiences **cultural value conflict**—torn between collectivist family norms and individualistic educational aspirations.

Intervention Strategies:

- **Cultural Humility Approach:** Explore her values without imposing Western individualism.
- **Narrative Therapy:** Help her reauthor her story to integrate both cultural identities.
- **Psychoeducation:** Normalize bicultural stress and promote bicultural competence.

Ethical Considerations:

- Avoid stereotyping or cultural bias.
- Respect family involvement while maintaining client autonomy.
- Address confidentiality carefully if family members request information.

Counselor Tip:
Ask open-ended questions like "What feels most important for you to honor about your culture?" instead of assuming cultural conflict means rejection of tradition.

6. Crisis and Emergency Cases

Case: "Jason's Breaking Point"

Background:
Jason, 28, was brought to the emergency department after telling a friend he "didn't see the point of living." He reports losing his job two weeks ago and ending a long-term relationship.

Assessment Focus:

- Immediate risk assessment (intent, plan, means, history)
- Protective factors and supports
- Substance use screening
- Mental health history

Conceptualization:
Jason is in **acute suicidal crisis** triggered by multiple losses and hopelessness.

Intervention Strategies:

- **Crisis Intervention Model (ABC):**
    - *A – Achieve rapport:* Create safety and trust.
    - *B – Boil down the problem:* Identify immediate

stressors.

    - *C – Cope actively:* Develop a short-term safety plan.

- **Safety Planning:** Identify coping skills, safe contacts, and remove lethal means.
- **Emergency Collaboration:** Involve crisis team or psychiatric evaluation if necessary.

Ethical Considerations:

- Duty to protect and break confidentiality if danger is imminent.
- Document all decisions and safety steps taken.
- Provide follow-up and continuity of care.

Counselor Tip:
Use calm, grounded language. Avoid "Why?" questions — focus on connection, not interrogation.

7. Substance Use and Co-Occurring Disorders

Case: "Tamika and the Cycle of Relapse"

Background:
Tamika, 41, has a history of alcohol dependence and depression. She's been sober for three months but recently relapsed after a conflict with her partner. She reports shame and self-blame.

Assessment Focus:

- Substance use history and triggers
- Co-occurring mood symptoms
- Relapse warning signs and supports
- Stage of change (motivation level)

Conceptualization:

Tamika exhibits a **co-occurring disorder** pattern: substance use as an emotional regulation tool for unresolved depression and interpersonal stress.

Intervention Strategies:

- **Integrated Dual Diagnosis Treatment (IDDT):** Address both substance use and mental health simultaneously.
- **Motivational Interviewing (MI):** Strengthen self-efficacy and explore ambivalence about sobriety.
- **Relapse Prevention Plan:** Identify triggers and coping alternatives.
- **Support Groups:** Encourage engagement with AA or SMART Recovery.

Ethical Considerations:

- Nonjudgmental stance to reduce shame.
- Respect autonomy while promoting safety.
- Collaborate with multidisciplinary team (psychiatrist, sponsor, therapist).

Counselor Tip:
Reframe relapse as a learning opportunity rather than a failure — use it to build insight and resilience.

8. Group Counseling Scenarios

Case: "The Anxiety Skills Group"

Background:
A weekly six-member group meets for stress and anxiety management. Members include college students and young professionals struggling with worry and perfectionism.

Common Themes:

- Social comparison and imposter syndrome

- Difficulty setting boundaries
- Overthinking and rumination

Group Process Focus:

- Establish psychological safety and confidentiality.
- Promote mutual empathy and shared learning.
- Manage group dynamics (dominant or withdrawn members).

Intervention Strategies:

- **CBT-Based Group Exercises:** Thought logs, behavioral experiments, relaxation training.
- **Psychoeducation:** Teach anxiety physiology and coping models.
- **Peer Feedback:** Use "I statements" and strengths-based sharing.

Ethical Considerations:

- Reinforce confidentiality agreements.
- Screen members carefully to ensure group readiness.
- Handle disclosure sensitively — avoid pressuring participants to share.

Counselor Tip:
Start each session with a brief check-in ("What's one stressor you managed this week?") to build connection and accountability.

9. Career and Vocational Cases

Case: "Derrick at a Crossroads"

Background:
Derrick, 29, recently completed his degree in marketing but

feels unfulfilled in his corporate job. He's considering switching careers to education but fears disappointing his parents and losing financial stability.

Assessment Focus:

- Career satisfaction and values alignment
- Personality, interests, and transferable skills
- External pressures and internal motivations
- Decision-making confidence

Conceptualization:
Derrick faces a **career indecision** rooted in value conflict — achievement and security vs. purpose and contribution.

Intervention Strategies:

- **Values Clarification:** Rank top five life priorities.
- **Career Assessments:** Use Holland Code (RIASEC) or StrengthsFinder to explore fit.
- **Decision Balance Sheet:** Evaluate gains/losses of each path.
- **Goal Setting:** Develop a 6-month exploration plan including informational interviews and volunteer experience.

Ethical Considerations:

- Avoid imposing counselor's career values.
- Maintain neutrality and confidentiality if parents are involved.
- Encourage realistic exploration without coercion.

Counselor Tip:
Normalize career transitions — the average person changes careers multiple times. Emphasize growth and adaptability over perfection.

Reflection and Practice

Use these reflection prompts to deepen your application of each scenario:

1. What immediate steps would you take in each case?
2. Which counseling models would best fit each population?
3. How would cultural, ethical, or systemic factors influence your approach?
4. What additional training or supervision might strengthen your competency in that area?

Summary

Effective counselors balance empathy, structure, and adaptability. These case studies demonstrate the art of tailoring interventions to unique client needs — from children facing anxiety to adults in crisis, couples in conflict, and diverse cultural backgrounds. Always approach each scenario with cultural humility, ethical awareness, and a growth mindset.

1. Children and Adolescents

Case Snapshot:
Lila, age 12, has recently begun refusing school and reports frequent stomachaches. Her parents are divorced, and communication between them is tense. Teachers describe her as "bright but withdrawn."

Conceptualization:
Lila's symptoms reflect anxiety with somatic features, likely influenced by family conflict and inconsistent parental communication.

Angle — What People Get Wrong:
Many counselors assume kids "can't articulate feelings," but with the right tools (art, play, drawing), children communicate clearly — just not verbally.

Pro Tip ?:
Use *externalizing language* ("It sounds like the worry monster visits you in the morning") to help children express emotion without shame.

Hidden Pitfall :
Avoid aligning with one parent. Even subtle biases can harm trust and violate ethical neutrality. Always communicate equally with both caregivers, unless safety concerns exist.

Techniques:

- Play-based emotional identification
- Family sessions to improve communication consistency
- School collaboration and structured morning routines

2. Adults

Case Snapshot:
Daniel, 35, presents with burnout symptoms — insomnia, irritability, loss of motivation. He's a high-performing manager with perfectionistic tendencies.

Conceptualization:
Adjustment disorder with anxious mood, rooted in unrealistic self-demands and poor work-life boundaries.

Angle — What People Get Wrong:
Burnout is not laziness or weakness — it's a *systemic imbalance* between demands and resources. Many adults mistake it for depression, leading to misdirected treatment.

Pro Tip :
Ask: *"What would rest look like if it didn't feel like failure?"* This redefines self-care for high achievers who equate rest with laziness.

Hidden Pitfall :
Don't rush to symptom management. Without addressing

perfectionism and identity-based worth, relief will be temporary.

Techniques:

- CBT cognitive restructuring around productivity beliefs
- Behavioral experiments (delegation, boundary-setting)
- Mindfulness and self-compassion training

3. Couples and Families

Case Snapshot:
Maria and Jorge seek counseling for "communication problems." They argue over finances and parenting but express mutual love.

Conceptualization:
Underlying dynamic: *pursuer–withdrawer cycle* common in attachment-based conflicts.

Angle — What People Get Wrong:
It's rarely about "communication skills." Most couples *can* communicate — the problem is *emotional safety.*

Pro Tip :
Before teaching "I-statements," establish emotional safety and curiosity:

> "Can you tell your partner what you most long for underneath the frustration?"

Hidden Pitfall :
Avoid becoming the referee. Counselors who "side" with logic over emotion often lose trust from both partners.

Techniques:

- Emotionally Focused Therapy (EFT) reframing
- Reflective listening and repair attempts
- Family systems mapping (roles, alliances, boundaries)

4. Older Adults and Aging Populations

Case Snapshot:
Ellen, 72, reports loneliness since her husband's death and increasing irritability toward her adult children.

Conceptualization:
Complicated grief and role transition; loss of identity as caregiver and partner.

Angle — What People Get Wrong:
Counselors sometimes over-pathologize sadness in older adults — confusing *grief* with *depression.* Sadness after loss is normal and healthy; it signals ongoing meaning-making.

Pro Tip :
Ask legacy-focused questions:

> "What parts of your husband's life or habits do you want to carry forward?"

This helps integrate memory with purpose.

Hidden Pitfall :
Avoid infantilizing clients — many older adults report feeling "talked down to" in therapy. Empower, don't protect.

Techniques:

- Life review therapy
- Meaning-centered interventions
- Peer or volunteer engagement plans

5. Multicultural and Diverse Populations

Case Snapshot:
Ahmed, a 27-year-old immigrant, feels isolated and anxious after relocating for work. He reports "feeling split between two worlds."

Conceptualization:
Acculturative stress and identity conflict, possibly intersecting with microaggressions and loss of community support.

Angle — What People Get Wrong:
Multicultural competence isn't just about "knowing cultures" — it's about *not assuming sameness.* Each person's cultural identity is unique and evolving.

Pro Tip :
Use the "ASK" method — **Ask, Seek, Know**:

- **Ask** what cultural values are most meaningful
- **Seek** to understand context before interpreting behavior
- **Know** your own assumptions before offering advice

Hidden Pitfall :
Avoid overcompensating with "cultural tokenism" (e.g., overly focusing on ethnicity or religion). It can alienate clients who wish to discuss universal struggles like belonging or purpose.

Techniques:

- Narrative therapy for identity reconstruction
- Strengths-based cultural reframing
- Community-based resources and advocacy

6. Crisis and Emergency Cases

Case Snapshot:
Tyler, 22, calls after a breakup, saying, "I don't want to be here anymore."

Conceptualization:
Acute situational crisis with suicidal ideation. Needs immediate safety assessment.

Angle — What People Get Wrong:
Asking about suicide does **not** plant the idea — it opens a

lifeline. Research shows direct inquiry *reduces* risk.

Pro Tip ?:
Ask directly but calmly:

> "Are you thinking about ending your life, or wishing you were dead?"

Then listen without panic — grounding calm helps stabilize the client.

Hidden Pitfall :
Don't rely on "no" as reassurance. Risk fluctuates. Reassess at every contact and document meticulously.

Techniques:

- Suicide risk assessment (plan, means, intent, history)
- Safety planning (use Worksheet 4)
- Involvement of supports and emergency protocols

7. Substance Use and Co-Occurring Disorders

Case Snapshot:
Ramon, 41, presents for anxiety but later discloses daily alcohol use "to unwind."

Conceptualization:
Co-occurring anxiety disorder and substance dependence — classic self-medication pattern.

Angle — What People Get Wrong:
Clients aren't "in denial" — they're protecting self-esteem and hope. The counselor's job is to *build motivation, not confrontation.*

Pro Tip ?:
Use *decisional balance worksheets*:

> "What do you like about drinking? What do you

dislike?"

This respects ambivalence and activates intrinsic motivation.

Hidden Pitfall :
Avoid rigid abstinence language early on; premature pressure often backfires. Meet the client's readiness stage (see Motivational Interviewing).

Techniques:

- Motivational interviewing
- CBT for cravings and triggers
- Relapse prevention planning

8. Group Counseling Scenarios

Case Snapshot:
A group of six adults in anger management class. Two members dominate; one remains silent.

Conceptualization:
Common group dynamic: power imbalance and role diffusion.

Angle — What People Get Wrong:
Group counseling isn't "six individual sessions at once." The *group itself* is the client. Interpersonal process is the real therapy.

Pro Tip ?:
At the start of each session, set one group goal ("Today we'll focus on listening, not fixing"). Reinforce group accountability.

Hidden Pitfall :
Don't rescue quiet members — forced participation breaks safety. Invite, but never demand.

Techniques:

- Process comments ("I notice the group goes quiet when anger comes up…")

- Use feedback loops and shared contracts
- End each session with "takeaway rounds"

9. Career and Vocational Cases

Case Snapshot:
Sophia, 28, feels "stuck" in a stable but unfulfilling accounting job. She worries about disappointing her family if she changes careers.

Conceptualization:
Existential conflict: values misalignment between external expectations and internal purpose.

Angle — What People Get Wrong:
Career counseling isn't only about résumés or aptitude — it's about **identity development**. Career crises are *life-stage crises in disguise.*

Pro Tip ?:
Use *values clarification* before job search exercises. Ask:

> "What would you regret not trying five years from now?"

Hidden Pitfall :
Avoid projecting your own career beliefs (e.g., "stability first") onto clients. Career counseling must be value-neutral.

Techniques:

- Holland Code exploration
- Narrative career construction
- SMART career goal planning

Pull-Out Section: Counselor Insight Box

> "The hardest thing for new counselors isn't mastering theory — it's managing the *emotional pace* of change.

Clients evolve unevenly; patience is as much a technique as any intervention."

Chapter 7: Essential Counseling Techniques and Interventions

Overview

Counseling techniques are the bridge between theory and practice.
While theories offer frameworks for understanding human behavior, **techniques** transform those ideas into concrete skills counselors use in the room — listening, questioning, reframing, and guiding clients toward change.

This chapter provides practical methods from major counseling approaches, crisis intervention models, and targeted techniques for specific issues.
Each section includes **"How-to Steps," "Sample Dialogue," and "Counselor Tips"** to help you master the art of applied counseling.

1. Core Skills Across Theoretical Orientations

A. Cognitive-Behavioral Therapy (CBT) Skills

Goal: Help clients identify, challenge, and change distorted thinking and maladaptive behaviors.

Key Techniques

1. **Cognitive Restructuring**
    - Identify automatic negative thoughts.
    - Examine evidence for and against them.
    - Replace with more balanced alternatives.

    Example:

    - Client: "I always fail at everything."

- Counselor: "Let's look at what 'always' means here. Can you recall a time you succeeded?"
- *Tip:* Use a thought record worksheet between sessions.

2. **Behavioral Activation**
   - Schedule pleasurable or mastery-oriented activities.
   - Reinforce positive mood-behavior connections.
3. **Exposure Techniques**
   - Gradually confront feared situations or memories.
   - Used in anxiety, trauma, or phobia treatment.
4. **Cognitive Rehearsal**
   - Practice coping thoughts or new behaviors before stressful situations.

Counselor Tip:
CBT works best when clients actively participate. Assign simple, realistic "homework" such as journaling, thought logs, or behavioral experiments.

B. Humanistic / Person-Centered Skills

Goal: Facilitate growth through empathy, authenticity, and unconditional positive regard.

Core Skills

1. **Active Listening**
   - Use eye contact, minimal encouragers ("I see," "Go on"), and open posture.
   - Focus fully on the client's message, not your next question.
2. **Reflection of Feelings**

- Mirror the emotional tone:
  "It sounds like you're really frustrated that your efforts aren't being recognized."

3. **Congruence (Genuineness)**
   - Be authentic and transparent, while maintaining professionalism.
4. **Empathic Understanding**
   - "You're trying so hard to stay positive, but it feels like no one notices."

Counselor Tip:
Presence often heals more than advice. Silence, empathy, and respect can be powerful interventions.

C. Psychodynamic and Insight-Oriented Techniques

Goal: Uncover unconscious patterns and unresolved conflicts influencing present behavior.

Key Techniques

1. **Exploration of Early Experiences**
   - "Tell me about what relationships were like growing up."
   - Look for themes repeating in current life.
2. **Interpretation**
   - Offer meaning behind behavior patterns.
     "It seems you distance yourself when someone gets too close — perhaps that protected you in the past."
3. **Transference and Countertransference Awareness**
   - *Transference:* Client projects feelings from past relationships onto counselor.

- *Countertransference:* Counselor's emotional reaction to client.
- Recognize and discuss these carefully to enhance insight.

4. **Free Association**
    - Encourage clients to verbalize thoughts without censorship to access unconscious material.

Counselor Tip:
Use insight gently. Timing matters — interpretations should clarify, not overwhelm.

D. Solution-Focused Brief Therapy (SFBT)

Goal: Build on client strengths and solutions instead of focusing on problems.

Core Techniques

1. **Miracle Question**
    - "If you woke up tomorrow and your problem was solved, what would be different?"
2. **Scaling Questions**
    - "On a scale of 0 to 10, how confident are you about handling this situation?"
3. **Exception Finding**
    - "Tell me about a time when this problem didn't happen."
4. **Compliments and Strength Reinforcement**
    - Acknowledge effort: "You've already taken important steps by seeking help."

Counselor Tip:

SFBT is ideal for short-term settings — schools, hospitals, or EAPs — where immediate change is prioritized.

E. Motivational Interviewing (MI)

Goal: Increase motivation for change by exploring ambivalence.

Core Principles (OARS)

- **O**pen Questions
- **A**ffirmations
- **R**eflections
- **S**ummaries

Example Dialogue:

> Counselor: "What are some things you like about drinking?"
> Client: "It helps me relax."
> Counselor: "And what are some things you don't like about it?"
> Client: "I hate how I feel the next day."
> Counselor: "So part of you enjoys the relaxation, but another part wants better mornings."

Counselor Tip:
Avoid confrontation. Evoke clients' own reasons for change — "You" statements motivate better than "You should."

F. Family Systems Techniques

Goal: Understand individual issues in the context of family dynamics and roles.

Key Tools

1. **Genograms:** Visual family maps showing relationships, conflicts, and patterns.
2. **Reframing:** Offer new perspectives on behaviors ("Your son isn't defiant — he's testing independence.")
3. **Boundary Setting:** Clarify enmeshment or disengagement.
4. **Circular Questioning:** "When your daughter gets quiet, how does your partner respond?"

Counselor Tip:
Always explore *interactional patterns*, not just individual behavior. Systems thinking sees the whole family as the client.

2. Crisis Intervention and Suicide Assessment

Crisis situations require swift, structured, and compassionate responses.
Crisis counseling prioritizes **stabilization, safety, and short-term coping**, not long-term insight.

A. Principles of Crisis Counseling

1. **Immediacy:** Respond as soon as possible.
2. **Safety:** Assess and ensure physical and psychological safety.
3. **Control:** Help the client regain a sense of mastery.
4. **Support:** Activate natural and community resources.
5. **Short-Term Focus:** Emphasize present coping and stabilization.

B. The ABC Model of Crisis Intervention

Step	Focus	Counselor Action
A – Achieve Rapport	Build trust and connection.	Use calm tone, open body language, validation.
B – Boil Down the Problem	Clarify the core issue.	Identify what led to the crisis and current coping capacity.
C – Cope Actively	Generate practical steps.	Develop safety plan, connect to supports, ensure follow-up.

C. Suicide Risk Assessment

Key Areas to Assess (Mnemonic: IS PATH WARM)

- **I**deation – Are there suicidal thoughts?
- **S**ubstance use – Any intoxication or abuse?
- **P**urposelessness – Feeling life has no meaning?
- **A**nxiety – Restlessness, agitation?
- **T**rapped – Feeling no escape?
- **H**opelessness – Belief things won't improve?
- **W**ithdrawal – Social isolation?
- **A**nger – Rage or seeking revenge?
- **R**ecklessness – Engaging in risky acts?
- **M**ood Changes – Sudden lift after depression (possible decision to die)?

Follow-up Questions:

1. "Have you had thoughts about wanting to die?"
2. "Do you have a plan for how you might harm yourself?"
3. "Do you have access to those means?"

4. “What’s kept you alive so far?”

Risk Level Guide:

Risk	Indicators	Action
Low	Fleeting thoughts, no plan	Continue therapy, develop safety plan
Moderate	Frequent thoughts, vague plan	Increase sessions, involve support system
High	Clear plan, means available	Do not leave alone; contact emergency services

D. Postvention and Follow-Up

After a crisis or suicide attempt:

- Schedule frequent check-ins.
- Coordinate with family, psychiatrist, or hospital staff.
- Debrief and support counselor self-care — crisis work can cause secondary trauma.

Counselor Tip:
Use a calm voice, move slowly, and avoid overpromising. Safety first — therapy later.

3. Techniques for Specific Issues

A. Substance Use

Common Goals: Build motivation, reduce harm, and promote recovery.

Effective Techniques

1. **Motivational Interviewing (MI):** Explore ambivalence and reinforce autonomy.
2. **Trigger Identification:** Use worksheets to track

situations, thoughts, or emotions that precede use.

3. **Urge Surfing:** Teach clients to ride cravings like waves — they rise and fall.
4. **Relapse Prevention Planning:** Identify warning signs early and rehearse coping responses.
5. **Support Group Integration:** Encourage attendance at AA, SMART Recovery, or culturally relevant groups.

Counselor Tip:
Never frame relapse as failure — it's data for future planning.

B. Grief and Loss

Goal: Facilitate healthy mourning, meaning-making, and adjustment.

Key Techniques

1. **Normalization:** Educate that grief responses vary — there's no single timeline.
2. **Storytelling and Life Review:** Invite clients to share memories and emotions.
3. **Symbolic Rituals:** Letter writing, lighting candles, or memorial activities.
4. **Empty Chair Exercise:** Speak to the deceased or estranged person to express unfinished emotions.
5. **Meaning Reconstruction:** Explore lessons, legacies, and identity changes post-loss.

Counselor Tip:
Avoid rushing closure. Grief isn't something to "get over," but to integrate into new meaning.

C. Anger Management

Goal: Help clients understand anger triggers, thoughts, and physiological responses.

Effective Techniques

1. **Anger Log:** Record situations, triggers, intensity, and reactions.
2. **Cognitive Reappraisal:** Challenge "should" or "must" beliefs fueling anger.
3. **Relaxation Training:** Deep breathing, progressive muscle relaxation, grounding.
4. **Timeouts and De-escalation Plans:** Walk away before escalation, set cool-down routines.
5. **Assertiveness Training:** Teach "I statements" for respectful self-expression.

Example:

Instead of "You never listen to me!"
Try: "I feel frustrated when I'm interrupted because I want to be heard."

Counselor Tip:
Normalize anger as a valid emotion; the goal is control, not suppression.

D. Anxiety Disorders

Goal: Reduce avoidance and retrain the nervous system's response to fear.

Core Techniques

1. **Psychoeducation:** Teach the anxiety cycle — thoughts → feelings → behaviors.

2. **Exposure Hierarchies:** Gradually face feared situations from least to most distressing.
3. **Relaxation & Breathing Techniques:** Diaphragmatic breathing, grounding.
4. **Cognitive Restructuring:** Identify catastrophizing or overgeneralization.
5. **Mindfulness Practice:** Observe thoughts without judgment.

Counselor Tip:
Remind clients: *The goal isn't to eliminate anxiety, but to learn that they can handle it.*

E. Depression

Goal: Increase activation, restructure negative beliefs, and rebuild purpose.

Key Techniques

1. **Behavioral Activation:** Plan daily small actions that create meaning or mastery.
2. **Cognitive Reframing:** Identify and challenge hopeless self-talk.
3. **Gratitude Journaling:** Track positive moments each day to shift attention.
4. **Values Work:** Help clients reconnect with what matters most.
5. **Interpersonal Repair:** Address loss, guilt, or role changes maintaining the depression.

Counselor Tip:
Start small — energy follows action. A 5-minute walk can begin to break inertia.

F. Trauma and PTSD

Goal: Reestablish safety, process trauma memories, and integrate new meaning.

Three-Stage Model

1. **Stabilization:** Safety, grounding, and emotion regulation.
2. **Processing:** Gradual exposure, narrative reconstruction, or EMDR (if trained).
3. **Integration:** Reconnecting with life, self, and relationships.

Grounding Techniques

- Name five things you see, four you touch, three you hear, two you smell, one you taste.
- Safe place visualization.
- Deep breathing or rhythmic tapping.

Counselor Tip:
Never rush trauma disclosure — stabilization must come first.

4. Integrating Techniques Across Theories

Effective counselors often **blend approaches** to match the client's needs.
For example:

- Combine CBT's structure with Humanistic empathy.
- Use MI for motivation, then CBT for skill-building.
- Apply systems thinking even in individual work (consider relational context).

Integration Formula:

Empathy (Humanistic) + Structure (CBT) +

Awareness (Psychodynamic) + Action (Behavioral) = Comprehensive Counseling

5. Practice Tools and Skill-Building Exercises

Skill Exercise 1: Reflection and Paraphrase Practice

- Watch or role-play a 10-minute client story.
- Practice reflecting both *content* and *feeling*.
- Debrief: What effect did reflection have on client openness?

Skill Exercise 2: Thought Record (CBT)

Situation	Emotion (0–100)	Automatic Thought	Evidence For	Evidence Against	Balanced Thought

Skill Exercise 3: Crisis Role-Play

Simulate a client in acute distress. Practice:

- Establishing safety
- Validating emotions
- Conducting risk assessment
- Creating immediate safety plan

Skill Exercise 4: Anger Trigger Chain

Event → Thought → Feeling → Behavior → Consequence
Help clients identify where they can intervene to break the cycle.

Chapter Summary

- Counseling techniques turn theory into transformation.
- Core skills — listening, reflection, goal-setting, and feedback — are universal.
- Tailor interventions to client readiness, culture, and context.
- Crisis and suicide work require calm, structured, and immediate safety measures.
- Specialized techniques (for grief, trauma, anger, or addiction) demand flexibility and empathy.
- The best counselors integrate multiple models rather than rigidly follow one.

1. Core Skills from Various Theoretical Orientations

(CBT, Humanistic, Psychodynamic, and More)

Overview

Effective counselors are flexible thinkers. They borrow from multiple theories — not as "mix and match," but as an integrated skillset guided by client needs.
The best counselors know *when* to use empathy, *when* to challenge, and *when* to stay silent.

A. Cognitive-Behavioral Techniques (CBT)

Purpose: Identify and reframe distorted thinking patterns that drive emotional distress and self-defeating behavior.

Key Tools:

- Cognitive restructuring

- Thought records
- Behavioral experiments
- Exposure hierarchies

Angle — What People Get Wrong:
CBT is not about "thinking positively." It's about *thinking accurately.* Counselors who push "just replace negative thoughts" often invalidate clients' real pain.

Pro Tip :
When helping clients reframe, start with *validation first*, correction second.

> "It makes sense you feel hopeless — anyone in your shoes would. Let's look together at what your thoughts are telling you."

Hidden Pitfall :
Avoid turning CBT into a worksheet factory. Real change happens in *discussion and discovery*, not checkboxes. If clients feel "quizzed," rapport collapses.

B. Humanistic and Person-Centered Techniques

Purpose: Facilitate growth through empathy, unconditional positive regard, and authenticity.

Core Skills:

- Reflective listening
- Congruence (authenticity)
- Unconditional positive regard

Angle — What People Get Wrong:
Many believe person-centered therapy is "just listening." In truth, *deep listening* is an active intervention — it dismantles shame and builds self-trust.

Pro Tip :
Silence can be a mirror. After a client's emotional statement, *pause three seconds*. That small gap often leads to deeper self-exploration.

Hidden Pitfall :
Avoid "performing empathy." Clients quickly sense inauthentic warmth. If you're not feeling it, ground yourself — authenticity matters more than politeness.

C. Psychodynamic Techniques

Purpose: Explore unconscious motives, past relationships, and unresolved internal conflicts.

Tools:

- Free association
- Dream and pattern exploration
- Transference and countertransference awareness

Angle — What People Get Wrong:
Psychodynamic therapy isn't outdated. Neuroscience supports its central claim: *the past shapes our present neural patterns.*

Pro Tip :
Track emotional "repeats." If a client reacts strongly to you — frustration, admiration, distrust — it's data, not disrespect. Explore, don't defend.

Hidden Pitfall :
New counselors often fear transference discussions. But avoiding them robs clients of insight. Address gently:

> "I wonder if how you feel toward me might resemble what happens with others in your life?"

D. Integrative and Eclectic Approaches

Purpose: Combine techniques from multiple orientations for customized care.

Angle — What People Get Wrong:
"Eclectic" doesn't mean random. Without theory behind each choice, eclecticism becomes chaos.

Pro Tip :
Ask yourself before using any tool: *What theory justifies this intervention right now?* If you can't answer, pause.

Hidden Pitfall :
Avoid switching styles too quickly. Clients need consistency to feel safe. Integration works best when gradual and explained.

2. Crisis Intervention and Suicide Assessment

Overview

Crisis work is not about *fixing* the crisis — it's about *slowing it down* and re-establishing safety. Counselors must act with both empathy and decisiveness.

A. Stages of Crisis Intervention

1. **Assess Risk:** Determine immediate danger or suicidal intent.
2. **Build Rapport:** Offer calm presence; reduce panic through tone and grounding.
3. **Identify Triggers:** Clarify what precipitated the crisis.
4. **Develop Coping & Safety Plan:** Involve supports, restrict access to means, set next steps.
5. **Follow-Up:** Reassess within 24–48 hours.

Angle — What People Get Wrong:
Asking about suicide does *not* increase risk — silence does.

Many trainees fear "saying the wrong thing," but the real danger is *not asking directly*.

Pro Tip :
Use clear, calm language:

> "Are you thinking of killing yourself, or wishing you were dead?"
> Directness saves lives; euphemisms create confusion.

Hidden Pitfall :
Never rely solely on your intuition. Document, consult, and follow protocol every time — especially with ambiguous or "low-risk" cases. Overconfidence is a common rookie trap.

B. Techniques for Grounding and Stabilization

Effective Tools:

- 5-4-3-2-1 grounding (sensory focus)
- Breathing retraining
- Crisis triage and referral mapping
- Safety contract or safety plan (see Worksheet 4)

Angle — What People Get Wrong:
You can't reason with someone in panic — the nervous system must be calmed first. Grounding comes *before* problem-solving.

Pro Tip :
When in doubt, slow your *own* breathing first. Clients mirror your rhythm unconsciously. Your calm is your most powerful de-escalation tool.

Hidden Pitfall :
Avoid false reassurance ("It'll be okay"). It invalidates fear. Replace with presence:

> "You're not alone right now. Let's breathe together and figure this out."

3. Techniques for Specific Issues

A. Substance Use

Core Interventions:

- Motivational Interviewing (MI)
- Relapse prevention planning
- Cognitive-behavioral craving management

Angle — What People Get Wrong:
Clients using substances aren't "resisting help" — they're *protecting relief*. The drug often represents their best-known coping mechanism.

Pro Tip ?:
Honor the function of the substance before removing it. Ask:

> "What does drinking do *for* you, not just *to* you?"

Hidden Pitfall :
Don't rush abstinence. Forcing premature sobriety often leads to relapse. Meet the client's readiness stage instead of demanding change.

B. Grief and Loss

Core Interventions:

- Meaning-making and narrative retelling
- Empty-chair or letter-writing exercises
- Continuing bonds model (maintaining symbolic connection)

Angle — What People Get Wrong:
Grief doesn't follow stages neatly. Kubler-Ross's model was *descriptive*, not prescriptive. Forcing "acceptance" creates shame around natural sorrow.

Pro Tip :
Invite permission to grieve:

> "What would your loved one say if they saw you taking time to heal today?"

Hidden Pitfall :
Avoid the "toxic positivity" trap — telling clients to "move on" or "find the silver lining." Validation is the medicine; time is the healer.

C. Anger Management

Core Interventions:

- Cognitive restructuring (triggers and beliefs)
- Relaxation and time-out techniques
- Communication training (assertiveness vs. aggression)

Angle — What People Get Wrong:
Anger isn't the problem — *unexpressed hurt* is. Anger is often the mask over fear, shame, or pain.

Pro Tip :
Ask clients:

> "If your anger could talk, what would it say it's protecting?"
> This reframes anger as a signal, not an enemy.

Hidden Pitfall :
Don't tell clients to "control" anger too early. Suppression increases pressure. Focus first on recognition, then regulation.

D. Anxiety and Panic

Core Interventions:

- Exposure hierarchy and desensitization

- Relaxation and breathing retraining
- Cognitive reframing of catastrophic thoughts

Angle — What People Get Wrong:
"Deep breathing" isn't always the first step. In panic, clients often *hyperventilate more* when told to "take deep breaths."

Pro Tip :
Coach **slower** breathing, not deeper. Try the 4–6 rhythm: inhale 4 seconds, exhale 6. Longer exhalation activates the parasympathetic system.

Hidden Pitfall :
Avoid challenging anxious thoughts too soon — first build tolerance to the body sensations. Insight without safety worsens panic.

E. Trauma and PTSD

Core Interventions:

- Grounding and stabilization before trauma exploration
- Narrative reconstruction
- Somatic awareness (tracking body cues)

Angle — What People Get Wrong:
Trauma work isn't about reliving the past — it's about reclaiming safety in the present. Many counselors re-traumatize clients by pushing disclosure too early.

Pro Tip :
Always ask consent before trauma retelling:

> "Would you like to talk about the event, or would it feel safer to stay focused on what's happening in your body right now?"

Hidden Pitfall :
Never start trauma exposure without a stabilization plan. If the

client leaves dysregulated, you've increased harm, not healing.

Pull-Out Box: Counselor Insight

> "The mark of an advanced counselor isn't using more techniques — it's using *fewer*, more precisely. Precision is compassion."

End-of-Chapter Summary

Every counseling technique — no matter how structured or simple — is only as effective as the counselor's presence behind it.
To practice effectively:

- Know what your method does and *why*
- Challenge myths kindly but confidently
- Watch for common traps of over-helping or under-boundarying

Remember: Counseling techniques are not mechanical scripts — they're languages of healing. Learn the grammar, but speak from the heart.

Chapter 8 : Practical Worksheets, Forms, and Templates

These practical tools are designed to help counselors, trainees, and supervisors apply the case scenarios to real-world counseling practice.
Each form can be photocopied, printed, or used digitally for reflection and planning.

Worksheet 1: Case Conceptualization Template

Purpose: To organize client information and guide treatment planning.

Section	Key Questions	Counselor Notes
Identifying Information	Name, age, gender, cultural background	
Presenting Problem	What brings the client to counseling? What symptoms or concerns are most distressing?	
History and Context	What significant life events, trauma, or patterns contribute to the current problem?	
Strengths and Resources	What internal/external supports does the client have?	
Theoretical Conceptualization	Which theory best explains this case (CBT, Family Systems, etc.)?	
Treatment Goals	What are the client's top 2–3 measurable goals?	
Intervention Plan	Which specific techniques	

Section	Key Questions	Counselor Notes
	or steps will address each goal?	
Cultural/Ethical Notes	What cultural values or ethical boundaries must guide your approach?	

Counselor Tip: Review and update this form after every 4–6 sessions to track progress and ensure alignment with client goals.

Worksheet 2: Session Planning & Reflection Log

Purpose: To help counselors plan and evaluate individual sessions for skill development.

Session #	Date	Goal for Session	Techniques Planned	Client Response	Counselor Reflection

End-of-Session Reflection Questions:

1. What went well today?
2. What challenges emerged?
3. What counselor skills were most effective?
4. What will you do differently next time?

Worksheet 3: Ethical Decision-Making Framework

Purpose: To ensure thoughtful and defensible decisions in complex ethical cases.

Step	Guiding Questions	Example Actions
1. Identify the Issue	What ethical principles are in conflict?	Confidentiality vs. Duty to Warn
2. Review Codes & Laws	Which professional codes apply (e.g., ACA,	Review Standard B.2.a –

Step	Guiding Questions	Example Actions
	APA)?	Confidentiality
3. Consult	Who can you consult for guidance (supervisor, ethics board)?	Supervisor or ethics hotline
4. Consider Options	What actions could you take?	Inform client, document risk, make referral
5. Evaluate Consequences	How will each action affect the client and others?	Balance harm vs. protection
6. Decide and Act	Choose the most ethical and least harmful path.	Document and follow through
7. Reflect	What did you learn for future practice?	Update protocols

Counselor Tip: Always document your decision-making process — clear documentation is your best ethical safeguard.

Worksheet 4: Crisis and Safety Planning Template

Purpose: To support immediate safety and stabilization in crisis counseling.

Client Name: ________________________
Date: ________________________
Counselor: ________________________

1. Warning Signs:

- Thoughts, feelings, behaviors that signal crisis onset:

2. Coping Strategies (Internal):

- Things I can do on my own to calm down (e.g., breathing, music, walk):

3. Social Support (External):

- People I can contact for help:
    - Name / Phone
    - Name / Phone

4. Professional Supports:

- Therapist / Counselor: ______________________________
- Crisis Hotline: ______________________________________
- Emergency Services: _________________________________

5. Safe Environment Plan:

- Remove or secure harmful items: _________________________
- Safe place to go: ______________________________________

6. Commit to Safety:
Client Signature: _________________________ Date: ____________

Worksheet 5: Multicultural Self-Reflection Inventory

Purpose: To promote cultural humility and awareness in counseling practice.

Rate yourself on a scale of 1 (low awareness) to 5 (high awareness).

Self-Reflection Statement	Rating (1–5)	Notes/Examples
I am aware of my own cultural values and biases.		
I actively seek to understand my client's worldview.		
I adapt interventions to respect cultural values.		
I check for language or communication barriers.		

Self-Reflection Statement	Rating (1–5)	Notes/Examples
I invite clients to educate me about cultural norms if appropriate.		
I include family/community values in treatment planning.		

Counselor Tip: Use this tool before and after sessions with culturally diverse clients to track personal growth.

Worksheet 6: Strengths and Solutions Map

Purpose: To shift focus from problems to solutions and resilience.

Client Name: ____________________
Primary Concern: ____________________

Strengths	Past Successes	Current Supports	New Solutions
What am I good at?	When have I overcome similar challenges?	Who helps me stay motivated?	What new strategies can I try?

Instructions:
Invite the client to co-create this table during a session. Use color markers or sticky notes to make it visual and collaborative.

? Worksheet 7: Group Counseling Participation Record

Purpose: To monitor group attendance, participation, and progress over time.

Member Name	Session Dates Attended	Participation Level (1–5)	Key Themes Shared	Progress/ Notes

Facilitator Notes:

- Track attendance trends and engagement.
- Use to identify members needing individual check-ins.
- Document themes emerging across sessions for continuity.

? Worksheet 8: Career and Values Clarification Exercise

Purpose: To help clients explore their personal and vocational direction.

Step 1 – List Your Top 10 Values:
(Examples: family, stability, creativity, service, independence)

Step 2 – Rank Your Top 5 Most Important Values:

1. ____________________
2. ____________________
3. ____________________
4. ____________________
5. ____________________

Step 3 – Career Alignment:

Value	Current Job Fit	Ideal Career Fit	Notes

Step 4 – Action Plan:

- Short-term goal (1–3 months): ____________________
- Long-term goal (6–12 months): ____________________

Counselor Tip: Encourage clients to discuss these values with mentors or family members to gain perspective before making major transitions.

? Worksheet 9: Grief and Life Review Journal

Purpose: To guide older clients or those experiencing loss in exploring meaning and legacy.

Prompt 1: What are three moments in your life that brought you deep pride or joy?

Prompt 2: What lessons would you want younger generations to learn from you?

Prompt 3: How can you honor the memory of someone you lost?

Prompt 4: What unfinished goals or dreams still hold meaning for you?

Prompt 5: What relationships or memories bring you the most comfort today?

Counselor Tip: Use this journal in grief groups or one-on-one life review sessions.

Worksheet 10: Case Review and Supervision Form

Purpose: To prepare for supervision and ensure ethical, reflective practice.

Topic	Notes
Client Code/Initials:	
Presenting Issue:	
Current Stage of Counseling:	
Challenges Encountered:	
Interventions Attempted:	

Topic	Notes
Client Response/Progress:	
Ethical or Cultural Issues:	
Questions for Supervisor:	
Next Steps:	

Supervisor Notes:

Counselor Tip: Keep this form updated weekly — it promotes accountability and supports continuous learning.

End of Chapter Summary

By applying the case studies and worksheets together, trainees develop integrated counseling skills — combining empathy with structure, ethical thinking with flexibility, and theory with real-world tools.
These templates can be used as:

- Classroom exercises
- Supervision materials
- Practice documentation guides
- Personal growth reflection

Chapter 9 : NCMHCE Scenario Set — Batch 1

(Questions 1–50)

? Case 1 — "I Can't Keep Up Anymore"

Client: Brianna, 29-year-old, accountant
Chief Complaint: Panic, overwhelming stress at work
History:

- 3 months: recurrent episodes w/ chest tightness, sweating, fear of dying
- ER visit normal cardiac exam
- Avoids driving on highways
- Drinks 2–3 glasses wine nightly
- No SI/HI
- GAD-7: 16 (Severe)
- Panic Disorder Severity Scale suggests panic w/ avoidance

Assessment Section

Q1. What is the MOST important first assessment area?
A. Explore trauma history
B. Assess frequency and triggers of panic attacks
C. Review family conflict
D. Discuss childhood attachment patterns
✅ **Correct: B** — functional assessment of presenting symptoms first.

Q2. Which assessment tool is MOST relevant to confirm diagnosis?
A. PCL-5
B. C-SSRS

C. Panic Disorder Severity Scale
D. Yale-Brown Obsessive Compulsive Scale
✅ **Correct: C**

Diagnosis Section

Q3. Most likely diagnosis?
A. Generalized Anxiety Disorder
B. Panic Disorder with Agoraphobia
C. Social Anxiety Disorder
D. Illness Anxiety Disorder
✅ **Correct: B** — highway avoidance suggests agoraphobia.

Q4. Which must be ruled out FIRST?
A. Bipolar disorder
B. Substance intoxication
C. Conduct disorder
D. Personality disorder
✅ **Correct: B** — medical/substance conditions always priority in anxiety presentations.

Treatment Planning

Q5. Initial MOST appropriate intervention?
A. Psychoeducation + breathing retraining
B. Psychodynamic analysis
C. Referral to inpatient care
D. Confront irrational beliefs aggressively
✅ **Correct: A**

Q6. What should be AVOIDED early on?
A. Gradual exposure
B. Hyperventilation management
C. Substance-use exploration
D. Intensive trauma processing
✅ **Correct: D** — unsafe destabilization.

Risk + Ethics

Q7. What is the counselor's BEST response to nightly alcohol use?
A. Refer immediately to detox
B. Ignore it
C. Screen risk + discuss coping alternatives
D. Recommend switching to beer
✅ **Correct: C**

Q8. Which legal issue is priority?
A. Mandated reporting
B. Duty to warn
C. Informed consent + documentation
D. Immigration status checks
✅ **Correct: C**

Progress Evaluation

Q9. Best short-term goal measure?
A. Self-esteem
B. Reduction in panic attacks per week
C. Childhood memories
D. Sleep dream content
✅ **Correct: B**

Q10. Expected timeframe for noticeable progress using CBT for panic?
A. 1–2 sessions
B. 4–12 sessions
C. 24–36 sessions
D. 52 sessions
✅ **Correct: B** — evidence-based CBT.

✅ **Case 1 Total Questions: 10**

Case 2 — "I Think They'd Be Better Without Me"

Client: Carlos, 46-year-old, male

Presenting: Severe depression, passive SI
Context: Recently divorced, missed work, 8 lb weight loss
PHQ-9 = 21 (Severe)
Reports vague suicidal thoughts without plan or means
Protective: strong attachment to daughter

Assessment

Q11. FIRST action?
A. Explore divorce details
B. Conduct structured suicide risk assessment
C. Begin insight-based therapy
D. Delay risk evaluation until rapport builds
✅ **Correct: B**

Q12. Most appropriate risk level classification?
A. No risk
B. Mild chronic
C. Moderate acute
D. Severe imminent
✅ **Correct: C** — passive SI + impairment.

Diagnosis

Q13. Likely diagnosis?
A. MDD, severe
B. Cyclothymic disorder
C. Persistent Depressive Disorder
D. Schizoaffective disorder
✅ **Correct: A**

Q14. Rule-out priority?
A. OCD
B. Psychotic features
C. Gambling disorder
D. Personality pathology
✅ **Correct: B**

Intervention

Q15. Intervention with **highest** immediate value?
A. Cognitive restructuring
B. Safety planning + close follow-up
C. Hypnosis
D. EMDR
✅**Correct: B**

Q16. Referral decision?
A. Automatic hospitalization
B. Co-management with PCP/psychiatry
C. Discontinue therapy
D. Only community support groups
✅**Correct: B**

Ethics

Q17. Documentation priority?
A. Favorite hobbies
B. Risk + protective factors
C. Therapist personal feelings
D. Astrological sign
✅**Correct: B**

Q18. Boundary risk?
A. Safety focus
B. Suggesting medication consult
C. Therapist offering rides to appointments
D. Weekly sessions
✅**Correct: C**

Progress

Q19. Most relevant measurement?
A. GAD-7
B. PHQ-9
C. Y-BOCS

D. DAST-10
✅**Correct: B**

Q20. How soon must counselor reassess SI?
A. Monthly
B. Next quarter
C. Every session
D. Only upon client request
✅**Correct: C**

✅**Case 2 Total Questions: 10**

? Case 3 — "Voices From the Past"

Client: Alicia, 33
Issue: Trauma history w/ auditory intrusions
Symptoms: Flashbacks, nightmares, hearing ex-husband yelling threats
Denies drug use
Hypervigilant, avoids men
PCL-5 score: 54 (Severe PTSD range)

Assessment

Q21. Counselor FIRST assesses:
A. Psychotic hallucination history
B. Trauma exposure + safety
C. Work performance
D. Sexual functioning
✅**Correct: B**

Q22. Key differential concern?
A. Schizophrenia
B. Borderline Personality Disorder
C. Panic Disorder
D. Somatic Disorder
✅**Correct: A** — rule out if voices trauma-related vs psychotic.

Diagnosis

Q23. Most likely?
A. PTSD with dissociative features
B. Schizoaffective disorder
C. Adjustment disorder
D. Malingering
✅ **Correct: A**

Q24. Which symptom confirms trauma linkage?
A. Fear of elevators
B. Flashbacks w/ specific abuser voice
C. Counting rituals
D. Weight gain
✅ **Correct: B**

Treatment

Q25. Best initial intervention?
A. EMDR reprocessing session 1
B. Grounding + stabilization
C. Confront cognitive distortions only
D. Psychodynamic dream analysis
✅ **Correct: B**

Q26. Timing of trauma exposure work?
A. Immediately
B. After stabilization + coping skills
C. Only last session
D. Never
✅ **Correct: B**

Ethics

Q27. Legal concern to monitor?
A. Self-disclosure
B. Abuser contact / stalking risk
C. Social media usage

D. Gym attendance
✅ **Correct: B**

Q28. Confidentiality limit to review?
A. Housing rules
B. Harm to self/others + DV reporting laws
C. Fashion choices
D. Therapist credentials
✅ **Correct: B**

Progress Tracking

Q29. Which scale best tracks trauma improvement?
A. PHQ-9
B. PCL-5
C. CAGE
D. AUDIT
✅ **Correct: B**

Q30. Expected PTSD progress timeframe?
A. 2–4 weeks
B. 6–20 weeks using TF-CBT
C. 1 year minimum
D. No recovery expected
✅ **Correct: B**

✅ **Case 3 Total Questions: 10**

? Case 4 — "Why Did They Fire Me?"

Client: Imani, 52
Concern: Irritability + job loss
Possible hypomania: ↑ talkativeness, ↓ sleep, impulsive spending
Family bipolar history
AUDIT score: 18 (Harmful use)

Assessment

Q31. First priority?
A. Evaluate alcohol impact
B. Debrief job loss emotions
C. Encourage journaling
D. Ask favorite color
✅ **Correct: A**

Q32. What tool is MOST relevant?
A. MOCA
B. AUDIT
C. Y-BOCS
D. C-SSRS
✅ **Correct: B**

Diagnosis

Q33. Most likely?
A. Bipolar II Disorder
B. Major Depressive Disorder
C. Panic Disorder
D. Gender Dysphoria
✅ **Correct: A**

Q34. MUST rule out first?
A. Thyroid condition
B. Attachment insecurity
C. Hoarding
D. Seasonal allergies
✅ **Correct: A**

Treatment

Q35. Best step?
A. Refer to psychiatry for medication evaluation
B. Only motivational interviewing
C. Yoga only

D. Assume symptoms are temporary
✅ **Correct: A**

Q36. Best counseling approach?
A. DBT only
B. Interpersonal process
C. Psychoeducation on mood tracking + sleep regulation
D. Exposure therapy
✅ **Correct: C**

Ethics

Q37. Dual diagnosis requires:
A. Treat alcohol only
B. Treat mood only
C. Integrated treatment + referrals
D. Ignore risk
✅ **Correct: C**

Q38. If client refuses psychiatry?
A. Terminate counseling immediately
B. Document refusal + continue motivational enhancement
C. Threaten hospitalization
D. Violate confidentiality
✅ **Correct: B**

Progress

Q39. Best measure for hypomania mood tracking?
A. Sleep logs + daily behavior chart
B. Dream journal
C. Horoscope reading
D. Daily selfies
✅ **Correct: A**

Q40. Timeframe for improvement after mood meds start?
A. Hours
B. 1–2 weeks minimum

C. 6 months
D. 2 years
✅**Correct: B**

✅**Case 4 Total Questions: 10**

Case 5 — "My Daughter Won't Listen"

Client: Janine (mother), brings daughter Zoe, 9
Concerns: School refusal, tantrums, nightmares
Father recently incarcerated
ACES score = 4 risk factors
Teacher notes anxiety around separation

Assessment

Q41. First priority?
A. Assess Zoe's safety + home stability
B. Discuss Janine's childhood
C. Replace coping with discipline
D. Change schools immediately
✅**Correct: A**

Q42. Which tool is MOST useful?
A. CAGE
B. SCARED (child anxiety rating)
C. Y-BOCS
D. MMPI-2
✅**Correct: B**

Diagnosis

Q43. Likely diagnosis?
A. ODD
B. Separation Anxiety Disorder
C. Autism Spectrum
D. Conduct Disorder
✅**Correct: B**

Q44. Another factor impacting functioning?
A. Parent incarceration trauma
B. Shoe style preference
C. Favorite games
D. Left-handedness
✅ **Correct: A**

Treatment

Q45. Best focus initially?
A. Family support + parenting strategies
B. Victim confrontation therapy
C. Interpret dreams
D. Touch therapy without consent
✅ **Correct: A**

Q46. Helpful school coordination?
A. Request truancy court
B. Sign ROI + collaborate w/ school counselor
C. Ignore school
D. Therapist visits home unannounced
✅ **Correct: B**

Ethics

Q47. Minor consent must include:
A. Candy rewards
B. Parent/guardian involvement
C. Zoe deciding alone
D. No documentation
✅ **Correct: B**

Q48. Mandatory reporting applies if:
A. Janine yells
B. Any suspected abuse/neglect
C. Parent is incarcerated
D. Child dislikes homework

✅ **Correct: B**

Progress

Q49. Best outcome indicator?
A. Reduced nightmares
B. Better phone privileges
C. Therapist opinion
D. Random mood changes
✅ **Correct: A**

Q50. Reassessment frequency for child anxiety?
A. At discharge only
B. Every 4–6 weeks
C. Annually
D. Never
✅ **Correct: B**

✅ **Case 5 Total Questions: 10**

✅ **Batch 1 Complete**

50 / 999 Questions
All written in **real NCMHCE scoring logic** format

Ready for Batch 2 (Questions 51–100)?

Before I generate the next chunk — quick preference check:

Do you want **increasing difficulty** over time?

A) Yes — make each set harder, more comorbid, ethical traps
B) Keep equal difficulty all the way through
C) Mix it randomly like real exam unpredictability

Just reply: **A**, **B**, or **C** ✅

NCMHCE Scenario Set — Batch 2 (Questions 51–100)

Case 6 — "Everyone Hates Me at School"

Client: Malik, 15
Presenting: Withdrawal, bullying victim, failing grades
History: Abrupt academic decline after peer cyberbullying
Reports feeling "numb" and "done with life"
C-SSRS: passive suicidal ideation without plan
No substance use
Limited peer supports

Assessment

Q51. MOST urgent assessment focus?
A. Orientation x3
B. Suicide risk + safety factors
C. Career goals
D. Video game habits
✅ **Correct: B**

Q52. Best tool to monitor depressive severity in teens?
A. PHQ-9 Modified for Teens
B. AUDIT
C. SCARED
D. OCI
✅ **Correct: A**

Diagnosis

Q53. Likely diagnosis?
A. DMDD
B. Major Depressive Disorder, current episode
C. Conduct Disorder
D. Autism Spectrum Disorder
✅ **Correct: B**

Q54. Key differential to rule out?

A. OCD
B. Trauma response from bullying
C. Eating disorder
D. Tourette's
✅ **Correct: B**

Treatment

Q55. Most appropriate early intervention?
A. Social skills training + CBT for depression
B. Psychoanalysis
C. Exposure to bullies
D. Recommend dropping out
✅ **Correct: A**

Q56. What else should clinician initiate?
A. Report school for negligence
B. School counseling collaboration with ROI
C. EMDR immediately
D. Encouraging isolation for safety
✅ **Correct: B**

Ethics / Legal

Q57. SI documentation MUST include:
A. Safety plan, protective factors, supervision
B. Political views
C. Clothing brand
D. Therapist mood
✅ **Correct: A**

Q58. Confidentiality with minors:
A. Break confidentiality only for immediate danger
B. Share every detail with parents
C. Allow teen to dictate all limits
D. Ignore parent involvement
✅ **Correct: A**

Progress

Q59. Best indicator of improvement?
A. More time online
B. Return to school engagement + mood lift
C. New hair style
D. Social media likes
✅ **Correct: B**

Q60. Reassessment of suicide risk should occur:
A. Monthly
B. Daily
C. At least weekly or each session
D. Only if he cries
✅ **Correct: C**

✅ **Case 6 Total: 10**

? Case 7 — "I Keep Checking the Stove"

Client: Lila, 34
Presenting: Intrusive worry fire will start
Compulsively checks appliances 30–50 times daily
Aware fear is irrational
Avoids guests to hide behaviors
Y-BOCS: elevated (Severe OCD)

Assessment

Q61. FIRST priority?
A. Rule out psychosis
B. Assess compulsions impact on functioning
C. Confront belief head-on
D. Ignore symptoms
✅ **Correct: B**

Q62. Which screening tool is most appropriate?
A. Y-BOCS
B. ACEs

C. AUDIT
D. MDQ
✅ **Correct: A**

Diagnosis

Q63. Best diagnosis?
A. OCPD
B. OCD with good insight
C. GAD
D. PTSD
✅ **Correct: B**

Q64. Must rule out:
A. Substance intoxication
B. Compensatory behaviors driven by trauma flashbacks
C. Personality disorder w/ perfectionism
D. Narcolepsy
✅ **Correct: C**

Treatment

Q65. Most effective intervention?
A. ERP (Exposure + Response Prevention)
B. Relaxation training only
C. Talk therapy about childhood
D. Threatening consequences for checking
✅ **Correct: A**

Q66. Poor early-phase treatment choice?
A. Tracking compulsions
B. Gradual exposure hierarchy
C. Forcing full exposure without rapport
D. Cognitive restructuring for obsessional fear
✅ **Correct: C**

Ethics

Q67. If client refuses ERP:
A. Document refusal + explore readiness
B. Terminate immediately
C. Inform employer
D. Insist on confrontation
✅ **Correct: A**

Q68. What is counselor's duty?
A. Maintain boundaries + evidence-based care
B. Guarantee cure
C. Provide daily home visits
D. Diagnose friends
✅ **Correct: A**

Progress

Q69. Best improvement indicator?
A. Reduction in compulsive checking frequency
B. Client buys new appliances
C. Moves to new home
D. Avoids stressors
✅ **Correct: A**

Q70. Typical ERP progress timeline?
A. 1–3 sessions
B. 8–20 sessions
C. 1 year minimum
D. No change expected
✅ **Correct: B**

✅ **Case 7 Total: 10**

Case 8 — "I Don't Trust You Either"

Client: Trey, 27
History: Long pattern of unstable relationships
Fear of abandonment

Self-harm threats when partner leaves
Mood swings triggered by rejection
C-SSRS: No plan, but recurrent gestures
ACEs score high

Assessment

Q71. Most relevant initial focus?
A. Evaluate self-harm risk + emotion regulation
B. Prioritize relationship reconciliation
C. Career counseling
D. Meditation only
✅ **Correct: A**

Q72. Useful assessment tool?
A. MSI-BPD
B. AUDIT
C. MOCA
D. CAPS
✅ **Correct: A**

Diagnosis

Q73. Most likely diagnosis?
A. Borderline Personality Disorder
B. Bipolar I
C. Narcissistic Personality Disorder
D. Panic Disorder
✅ **Correct: A**

Q74. Key differential to rule out due to mood swings?
A. Specific phobia
B. Bipolar disorder symptoms independent of relationships
C. Tourette's
D. ADHD
✅ **Correct: B**

Treatment

Q75. Best treatment modality?
A. DBT
B. Couples therapy only
C. Hypnosis
D. Confrontation of personality traits
✅ **Correct: A**

Q76. Crisis intervention plan should include:
A. Safety planning + DBT skills coaching
B. Threatening hospitalization
C. Ignoring self-harm statements
D. Telling client to "grow up"
✅ **Correct: A**

Ethics / Legal

Q77. Self-harm disclosure requires:
A. Risk evaluation + documentation
B. Report to employer
C. Inform family without consent automatically
D. Therapist jokes to lighten mood
✅ **Correct: A**

Q78. Confidentiality breach justified if:
A. Imminent self-harm danger
B. Client yells once
C. Therapist fears abandonment
D. Client lies
✅ **Correct: A**

Progress

Q79. Short-term treatment goal?
A. Increase emotional regulation skills
B. Achieve perfect stability
C. Eliminate all conflict

D. Diagnose partner
✅**Correct: A**

Q80. Expected improvement timeline with DBT?
A. Overnight
B. 6–12 months
C. 10 years
D. No improvement possible
✅**Correct: B**

✅**Case 8 Total: 10**

Case 9 — "I'm Gonna Lose My Kids"

Client: Marie, 39
Presenting: CPS involvement due to neglect report
Symptoms: fatigue, low motivation, overwhelmed
PHQ-9 = 18 (Moderately Severe)
AUDIT: 20 (problematic drinking)
2 young children at home

Assessment

Q81. First priority?
A. Explore CPS case requirements
B. Assess child safety + environment
C. Process shame
D. Focus solely on alcohol
✅**Correct: B**

Q82. Tool for substance screening?
A. AUDIT
B. SCARED
C. MMPI-A
D. PANSS
✅**Correct: A**

Diagnosis

Q83. Likely diagnosis?
A. Major Depressive Disorder + Alcohol Use Disorder
B. Schizophrenia
C. ADHD
D. OCD
✅ **Correct: A**

Q84. Risk factor raising removal risk?
A. Social support loss
B. New hobby
C. Outdoor exercise
D. Excessive optimism
✅ **Correct: A**

Treatment

Q85. MOST appropriate approach?
A. Integrated treatment: depression + SUD
B. Only CBT for depression
C. Only AA
D. Terminate services
✅ **Correct: A**

Q86. Community resource referral?
A. Parenting support + intensive outpatient program
B. Polygraph testing
C. Tattoos to boost confidence
D. Send kids away permanently
✅ **Correct: A**

Ethics

Q87. What must counselor document?
A. Safety issues, CPS communication, client compliance
B. Client's political views
C. Therapist's favorite intervention

D. Future arrest predictions
✅**Correct: A**

Q88. When is reporting mandated?
A. Any reasonable suspicion of neglect
B. When client admits gambling
C. If client argues
D. If therapist doesn't like client
✅**Correct: A**

Progress

Q89. Best indicator of improvement?
A. Children's needs reliably met + decreased substance use
B. More excuses
C. Avoids CPS
D. Stops coming to therapy
✅**Correct: A**

Q90. Frequency of reassessment for risk?
A. At discharge only
B. Weekly or as change occurs
C. Yearly
D. Never
✅**Correct: B**

✅**Case 9 Total: 10**

? Case 10 — "It's Like They're Watching Me"

Client: Devin, 22
Chief: Believes neighbors are spying
Isolating in basement
Increased suspiciousness 6 months
No substance use
Family history: Schizophrenia in father
MSE: Guarded, delusional ideation

Assessment

Q91. MOST immediate assessment need?
A. Reality testing + rule out threat to others
B. Employment history
C. Birth order
D. Romantic relationships
✅ **Correct: A**

Q92. Priority to rule out?
A. Organic/medical causes (neurological)
B. Fear of dogs
C. Simple phobia
D. Dyslexia
✅ **Correct: A**

Diagnosis

Q93. Most likely diagnosis?
A. Delusional Disorder, Persecutory Type
B. MDD
C. GAD
D. Somatic Symptom Disorder
✅ **Correct: A** (6 months, functioning mostly intact)

Q94. Differential to distinguish from schizophrenia:
A. Level of disorganized behavior + negative symptoms
B. Favorite music
C. Social media use
D. Travel history
✅ **Correct: A**

Treatment

Q95. Most appropriate step?
A. Refer to psychiatry for antipsychotic evaluation
B. Challenge delusion aggressively
C. Ignore symptoms

D. Encourage belief validation
✅ **Correct: A**

Q96. Initial therapy focus?
A. Therapeutic alliance + coping skills
B. Confront paranoia
C. Mind reading
D. Trauma exposure
✅ **Correct: A**

Ethics

Q97. Documentation must reflect:
A. Mental status findings + risk
B. Counselor frustrations
C. Musical tastes
D. Personal political thoughts
✅ **Correct: A**

Q98. Disclosure is required if:
A. Threats escalate to harm potential
B. Client skips session
C. Therapist dislikes client
D. Diagnosis is stigmatized
✅ **Correct: A**

Progress

Q99. Best progress indicator?
A. Reduced conviction in paranoia + increased functioning
B. More isolation
C. Increased surveillance behavior
D. Heightened fear
✅ **Correct: A**

Q100. Follow-up schedule after med referral?
A. 6 months later
B. Coordinate care + frequent check-ins (weekly/biweekly)

C. Discharge
D. Monthly only
✅ **Correct: B**

✅ **Case 10 Total: 10**
✅ Batch 2 Complete: **Questions 51–100**

✅ Batch 3 — Questions 101–150

NCMHCE Clinical Scenarios (Decision-Based with Answers)

Vignette 101–105 — Adolescent Mood + Risk

Client: 16-year-old male referred by school counselor for escalating irritability, skipping classes, and recent breakup. Mother reports increased sleep and "locking himself in his room." Grades dropped from B's to D's in 2 months. Denies substance use.
PHQ-9 score: **17** (moderately severe depression)
Columbia-Suicide Severity Rating Scale: **Passive SI** without plan.

101. What is the FIRST clinical priority?
A. Conduct a strengths assessment
B. Begin cognitive restructuring
C. Complete full suicide risk assessment
D. Ask about parental discipline strategies
Answer: C

102. What is the MOST appropriate initial intervention?
A. Create safety plan with client and mother
B. Refer immediately to inpatient hospitalization
C. Couples counseling for parents
D. Wait to address SI later in treatment
Answer: A

103. Based on symptoms and impairment, most likely diagnosis?
A. Persistent Depressive Disorder

B. Disruptive Mood Dysregulation Disorder
C. Major Depressive Disorder
D. Cyclothymic Disorder
Answer: C
(episodic, ≥2 weeks, functional decline)

104. What additional evaluation is MOST important for differential?
A. ADHD screener
B. Urine drug screen
C. Trauma history and bullying assessment
D. Autism assessment
Answer: C

105. Which referral BEST supports stabilization?
A. Group therapy only
B. Medication evaluation with child psychiatrist
C. Art therapy via community center
D. Truancy court intervention
Answer: B

Vignette 106–110 — Domestic Violence Safety

Client: 32-year-old woman reports emotional abuse and increased controlling behavior from partner. Visible bruise on upper arm. She states, "I can handle it. It's my fault sometimes." She fears losing their kids if she leaves.

106. What is the FIRST step?
A. Educate on power dynamics
B. Complete lethality risk assessment
C. Confront partner in session
D. Provide couples counseling referral
Answer: B

107. Most appropriate intervention at this stage?
A. Mandate separation
B. Develop a safety plan discreetly

C. Teach communication skills with partner
D. Encourage forgiveness work
Answer: B

108. Ethical action?
A. Contact CPS immediately for emotional abuse
B. Explain limits of confidentiality clearly
C. Subpoena partner for evaluation
D. Refuse treatment unless partner attends
Answer: B

109. Client expresses intent to leave soon. Best referral?
A. Shelter services and DV advocacy
B. Couples counseling to support transition
C. Budgeting workshop
D. Parenting class
Answer: A

110. If she insists it's partly her fault… best response:
A. Challenge distorted belief with psychoeducation
B. Avoid addressing abuse until rapport stronger
C. Agree it is mutual
D. Call police without consent
Answer: A

Vignette 111–115 — Psychosis + Cultural Competence

Client: 27-year-old Haitian man reports hearing male voices speaking in Creole, "encouraging him to be strong." No commands. Family describes spiritual experience. No safety concerns.

111. FIRST priority action?
A. Determine command hallucinations
B. Diagnose Schizophrenia immediately
C. Challenge cultural beliefs
D. Refer to inpatient unit
Answer: A

112. Helpful culturally competent step?
A. Contact spiritual leader (with consent)
B. Ignore cultural explanation
C. Label voices as delusion
D. Provide medication without assessment
Answer: A

113. Most likely diagnosis to explore initially?
A. Brief Psychotic Disorder
B. Schizophrenia
C. Schizoaffective Disorder
D. Cultural idiom of distress / non-pathological
Answer: D

114. Which tool helps functional assessment?
A. Beck Anxiety Inventory
B. WHODAS 2.0
C. CAGE
D. Autism Diagnostic Observation Schedule
Answer: B

115. Risk escalates if:
A. Voices provide comfort
B. Social support is strong
C. Voices become commanding
D. Client attends religious ceremonies
Answer: C

Vignette 116–120 — PTSD + Substance Use

Client: 38-year-old veteran, hypervigilance, nightmares, daily alcohol use (6–8 beers). Avoids crowds. No suicidal ideation but "dangerous driving" when triggered.

116. First treatment focus per NCMHCE scoring?
A. Reduce trauma thoughts immediately
B. Stabilization + reduce substance use risk
C. EMDR in first session

D. Couples therapy
Answer: B

117. Most likely diagnosis?
A. Acute Stress Disorder
B. Substance-Induced Anxiety
C. PTSD w/ comorbid Alcohol Use Disorder
D. Generalized Anxiety Disorder
Answer: C

118. Appropriate referral?
A. Dual-diagnosis program
B. Solo grief therapy
C. Family estrangement workshop
D. Medication for sleep only
Answer: A

119. Best early intervention?
A. Exposure therapy immediately
B. Grounding + coping skills
C. Encourage increasing alcohol to sleep
D. Force trauma narrative
Answer: B

120. Functional safety concern?
A. Avoiding fireworks
B. Increased alcohol + risk behaviors
C. Asking for grounding tools
D. Healthy support system
Answer: B

Vignette 121–125 — ADHD vs Bipolar II Differential

Client: 29-year-old female. Distractibility, impulsive online shopping, fluctuating sleep (3–10 hours), episodes of intense productivity lasting 3 days, followed by fatigue and guilt. No psychosis.
Mood tracking suggests cyclical changes monthly.

121. Most important differential feature?
A. Concentration issues
B. Childhood onset history
C. Amount of coffee consumed
D. Cash flow stability
Answer: B (supports ADHD if present since childhood)

122. Best initial dx focus?
A. Bipolar II Disorder
B. ADHD
C. Borderline Personality Disorder
D. Intermittent Explosive Disorder
Answer: A (episodic hypomanic + depressive features)

123. Which tool helps diagnostic clarity?
A. Mood charts & collateral information
B. Alcohol screening only
C. IQ testing
D. Trauma checklist only
Answer: A

124. First intervention priority?
A. Stabilize mood cycles
B. Prevent shopping
C. Couples therapy
D. Limit caffeine
Answer: A

125. Which referral aligns with best practice?
A. Psychiatric evaluation for mood stabilizer
B. Herbal supplements
C. Hypnosis
D. Credit counseling only
Answer: A

Vignette 126–130 — Suicidal Client in Relapse

Client: 42-year-old male with history of opioid use disorder.

Recently fired, endorses SI with plan “to overdose.” States he has enough pills to do it. No protective factors identified.

126. Immediate priority?
A. Identify triggers for relapse
B. Activate emergency services/involuntary hospitalization
C. Resume CBT homework
D. Suggest exercise routine
Answer: B

127. Risk severity level?
A. Mild
B. Moderate
C. High
D. Low
Answer: C (plan + means + intent)

128. Next appropriate step?
A. Continue outpatient therapy tomorrow
B. Conduct commitment paperwork
C. Recommend journaling
D. Explore spirituality
Answer: B

129. After stabilization, key treatment focus?
A. Reinforce relapse analysis and MAT options
B. Exposure therapy for trauma
C. Avoid discussing drug history
D. Encourage independent detox
Answer: A

130. Evidence-based intervention?
A. Motivational Interviewing + MAT
B. Aromatherapy alone
C. Cyberbullying intervention
D. Psychoanalysis alone
Answer: A

Vignette 131–135 — Eating Disorder + Medical Risk

Client: 21-year-old college student, BMI 16.1, exercises 2–3 hours daily, laxative misuse. Denies SI. Reports dizziness and hair loss.

131. Immediate clinical decision?
A. Continue outpatient CBT weekly
B. Urgent medical evaluation + multidisciplinary care
C. Assign food journal only
D. Focus on career goals
Answer: B

132. Best-fitting diagnosis?
A. ARFID
B. Bulimia Nervosa
C. Anorexia Nervosa, restricting type
D. Binge Eating Disorder
Answer: C

133. Safety concern?
A. Social withdrawal
B. Hair styling changes
C. Cardiac complications / electrolyte imbalance
D. Difficult roommate
Answer: C

134. Ethical issue?
A. Confidentiality limits if life-threatening
B. Decor choices in office
C. Client clothing style
D. Age difference with counselor
Answer: A

135. Helpful early goal?
A. Weight restoration + normalized eating patterns
B. Increase workouts safely
C. Family blame reprocessing
D. Achieve visible abs

Answer: A

Vignette 136–140 — OCD vs Psychosis

Client: 30-year-old accountant with distressing thoughts of stabbing coworkers. No intent, fear of acting on thought, rituals include checking knives repeatedly.

136. FIRST diagnostic focus?
A. Suicidal ideation
B. Obsessions vs delusions
C. Trauma history
D. Parenting skills
Answer: B

137. Most likely diagnosis?
A. Psychotic Disorder
B. OCD
C. Antisocial Personality Disorder
D. Homicidal ideation intent
Answer: B

138. First-line treatment?
A. Exposure and Response Prevention
B. Couples counseling
C. Hypnotherapy
D. Aromatherapy
Answer: A

139. Ethical concern?
A. Mandatory report of intrusive thoughts
B. Assess risk of actual harm
C. Report employer
D. Label client as dangerous
Answer: B

140. Helpful intervention language?
A. Normalize intrusive thoughts
B. Confirm thoughts indicate violence

C. Encourage knife avoidance forever
D. Suggest client quit job
Answer: A

Vignette 141–145 — Co-Parenting Conflict

Client: Recently divorced parents in high conflict. Court-ordered therapy. Sessions become arguments. No safety concerns.

141. Primary function of therapy?
A. Relationship reconciliation
B. Co-parenting skill development
C. Financial planning
D. Child custody decisions
Answer: B

142. FIRST step when arguments escalate?
A. Pause session & reestablish boundaries
B. Encourage arguing to release tension
C. Side with one parent
D. Terminate therapy immediately
Answer: A

143. Best intervention?
A. Parallel parenting structure
B. Psychoanalysis on childhood trauma
C. Couples intimacy exercises
D. Ignore court guidelines
Answer: A

144. Ethical risk?
A. Dual agency if treating each individually
B. Discussing parenting
C. Scheduling morning sessions
D. Allowing venting
Answer: A

145. Documenting sessions must include:

A. Who is “right” in conflict
B. Neutral, child-focused clinical goals
C. Political beliefs
D. Therapist opinions about custody
Answer: B

Vignette 146–150 — Panic Disorder vs Cardiac Issues

Client: 50-year-old woman, sudden chest pain, sweating, fear of dying, ER ruled out heart disease last week. Avoids driving now.

146. Diagnosis most likely?
A. Panic Disorder
B. Somatic Symptom Disorder
C. Illness Anxiety Disorder
D. Delusional Disorder
Answer: A

147. FIRST clinical action?
A. Breathing & grounding skills
B. Confront avoidance harshly
C. Advice to stop seeking medical care
D. Suggest herbal remedies only
Answer: A

148. Functional risk?
A. Avoiding driving affecting work
B. Enjoying gardening
C. Using coping strategies
D. Strong family support
Answer: A

149. Helpful assessment tool?
A. Panic Disorder Severity Scale (PDSS)
B. CAGE
C. Child trauma screener
D. Autism measure
Answer: A

150. Long-term intervention?
A. Gradual exposure to avoided situations
B. Encourage complete avoidance
C. Medication only
D. Family therapy only
Answer: A

✅ Batch 4 — Questions 151–200

NCMHCE Clinical Scenarios (Decision-Based with Answers)

Vignette 151–155 — Child Trauma & Reporting Duty

Client: 9-year-old girl referred by school counselor after saying her stepfather "touches me sometimes and says it's our secret." Appears anxious, avoids eye contact, clutches stuffed toy.

151. FIRST action by counselor?
A. Ask for detailed timeline
B. Report suspected abuse to CPS
C. Conduct trauma narrative
D. Wait to see if she repeats claim
Answer: B *(Mandated reporting immediately)*

152. After reporting, next appropriate step?
A. Confront stepfather
B. Provide trauma-informed stabilization
C. Discuss legal consequences with child
D. Ask mother if she's aware
Answer: B

153. Best initial diagnosis likely?
A. Reactive Attachment Disorder
B. PTSD (provisional)
C. Oppositional Defiant Disorder
D. ADHD
Answer: B

154. What must documentation include?

A. Exact words from child
B. Therapist's assumptions
C. Legal opinions
D. Custody recommendations
Answer: A

155. Ethical requirement?
A. Inform school not to contact CPS
B. Maintain safety + minimize retraumatization
C. Allow stepfather to attend sessions
D. Delay therapy until case closes
Answer: B

Vignette 156–160 — College Anxiety + Perfectionism

Client: 20-year-old biology student. Panic attacks before exams, excessive studying (10–12 hrs/day), all-or-nothing thinking. No SI.

156. Likely diagnosis?
A. Panic Disorder
B. GAD with Panic Attacks
C. OCD
D. Social Anxiety Disorder
Answer: B

157. First-line intervention?
A. ERP
B. CBT for anxiety + cognitive restructuring
C. Existential exploration of destiny
D. Sleep restriction
Answer: B

158. What would be the MOST helpful coping strategy?
A. Cancel exams
B. Scheduled breaks + study coping plan
C. Drop out of school
D. Overprepare aggressively

Answer: B

159. Which symptoms require further medical rule-out?
A. Breathlessness + chest pain
B. Fear of failure
C. High effort studying
D. Crying after low grades
Answer: A

160. Helpful long-term strategy?
A. Exposure to test environments
B. Avoid exams
C. Medicate without therapy
D. Increase perfectionism
Answer: A

Vignette 161–165 — Borderline Personality + Crisis Work

Client: 25-year-old woman, unstable relationships, chronic emptiness, SI during conflicts, self-harm history (cutting). Frequent ER visits.

161. Most appropriate diagnosis?
A. Bipolar I
B. Borderline Personality Disorder
C. Histrionic PD
D. Avoidant PD
Answer: B

162. FIRST treatment priority?
A. Processing childhood trauma
B. Crisis safety stabilization
C. Couples therapy
D. Medication only
Answer: B

163. Evidence-based intervention of choice?
A. DBT
B. Psychoanalysis only

C. Confrontation therapy
D. EMDR as first step
Answer: A

164. Best therapeutic stance?
A. Firm boundaries + validation
B. Overinvolvement to build trust
C. Challenge client aggressively
D. Focus solely on positive thinking
Answer: A

165. Ethical note?
A. Collaborative safety planning is essential
B. Therapist decides boundaries alone
C. Always conduct therapy via text
D. Terminate immediately when distressed
Answer: A

Vignette 166–170 — Autism vs Social Anxiety Differential

Client: 14-year-old boy. Extreme discomfort with peers, rigid routines, literal speech, misreads sarcasm. No bullying history.

166. Most likely diagnostic focus?
A. Conduct Disorder
B. Autism Spectrum Disorder
C. Bipolar Disorder
D. Panic Disorder
Answer: B

167. Functional impact assessment tool?
A. WHODAS 2.0
B. CAGE
C. Beck Depression Inventory
D. C-SSRS
Answer: A

168. Parent asks "Did we cause this?" Best response:
A. Validate feelings + provide education

B. Blame genetics only
C. Ignore question
D. Tell them to research alone
Answer: A

169. School-based support referral?
A. IEP / Social skills group
B. Military recruitment
C. Jury duty exemption
D. Punishment-based discipline
Answer: A

170. First treatment goal?
A. Enhanced communication + coping skills
B. Cure autism
C. Full independence immediately
D. Remove electronics entirely
Answer: A

Vignette 171–175 — Bipolar I High-Risk Mania

Client: 40-year-old male with Bipolar I, not sleeping 4 days, pressured speech, grandiosity ("I'm chosen to save the world"). Spent $20,000 recently.

171. Immediate risk action?
A. Safety + hospitalization referral
B. Journaling
C. Allow financial decisions
D. Debate delusions
Answer: A

172. Risk level?
A. Mild
B. Moderate
C. High
D. Minimal
Answer: C

173. Which symptoms indicate need for rapid intervention?
A. Creative ideas
B. Decreased need for sleep + risky spending
C. Healthy appetite
D. Feeling confident
Answer: B

174. Collaboration?
A. With psychiatrist on medication stabilization
B. Only treat with therapy
C. Encourage independent recovery
D. Quit therapy
Answer: A

175. Avoid?
A. Confronting delusions aggressively
B. Safety assessment
C. Family collateral (w/ consent)
D. Crisis referral
Answer: A

Vignette 176–180 — LGBTQ+ Youth + Family Conflict

Client: 17-year-old trans girl, parents rejecting identity. Passive SI but no plan. Isolated at home, grades declining.

176. FIRST clinical priority?
A. Family therapy
B. Assess suicidality and support safety
C. Persuade parents to accept
D. Explore career goals
Answer: B

177. Most affirming supportive intervention?
A. Encourage hiding identity
B. Connection to LGBTQ+ youth groups
C. Rely on parents to manage care
D. Suggest ignoring gender dysphoria

Answer: B

178. Ethical stance?
A. Advocate for client's access to safe care
B. Break confidentiality to enforce acceptance
C. Avoid discussing gender topics
D. Tell parents the client is confused
Answer: A

179. Diagnosis to consider?
A. Gender Dysphoria
B. Schizoaffective Disorder
C. Antisocial Personality Disorder
D. Kleptomania
Answer: A

180. Best documentation focus?
A. Suicide risk & protective factors
B. Therapist opinion on politics
C. Client fashion choices
D. Family finances
Answer: A

Vignette 181–185 — Grief vs Major Depression

Client: 34-year-old man. Lost spouse 3 months ago. Sadness, insomnia, guilt, passive wish to "sleep forever," but values his children.

181. Key differential for MDD vs grief?
A. Missing loved one
B. Preserved self-worth
C. Crying
D. Sadness triggered by memories
Answer: B *(if guilt > self-worth → MDD)*

182. FIRST treatment approach?
A. Validate grief; normalize emotions
B. Push dating immediately

C. Diagnose premature MDD
D. Remove home memories
Answer: A

183. Safety consideration?
A. Columbia Suicide Severity Scale
B. IQ testing
C. Fitness tracking
D. Personality assessment only
Answer: A

184. Referral if symptoms worsen?
A. Psychiatric med evaluation
B. High-intensity exercise plan
C. Ignore concerns
D. Quit therapy until "over it"
Answer: A

185. Intervention for coping?
A. Grief support group
B. Prolonged isolation
C. Avoid discussing spouse
D. Punitive self-criticism
Answer: A

Vignette 186–190 — Conduct Disorder + Legal Risk

Client: 15-year-old male. Stealing, truancy, aggressive behavior, lack of remorse. Court involved.

186. Likely diagnosis?
A. Oppositional Defiant Disorder
B. Conduct Disorder
C. Intermittent Explosive Disorder
D. Autism
Answer: B

187. FIRST priority?
A. Risk management + safety

B. Career planning
C. Meditation
D. Short-term termination
Answer: A

188. Systemic approach?
A. Multisystemic Therapy (MST)
B. Aromatherapy
C. Yoga only
D. Self-therapy
Answer: A

189. Family engagement helps:
A. Consistent boundaries + supervision
B. Allowing more freedom
C. Removing consequences
D. Ignoring behavior
Answer: A

190. Progress measure?
A. School attendance & behavioral tracking
B. Self-diagnosis
C. Daily social media posting
D. Peer popularity
Answer: A

Vignette 191–195 — Alzheimer's vs Depression in Older Adult

Client: 72-year-old woman. Forgetful, withdrawing socially, slow speech, poor appetite. Onset after spouse died.

191. Key differential clue?
A. Sudden onset after stressor → depression
B. Forgetting minor details
C. Age over 70
D. Low appetite
Answer: A

192. FIRST step?
A. Screen for depression & cognitive impairment
B. Assume dementia
C. Ignore concerns
D. Terminate treatment
Answer: A

193. Tool for cognitive screening?
A. MoCA or MMSE
B. PTSD Checklist
C. AUDIT
D. Autism Screener
Answer: A

194. If depression confirmed, best intervention?
A. Behavioral activation
B. Online gaming
C. Hypnosis only
D. Immediate nursing home placement
Answer: A

195. Safety consideration?
A. Medication adherence monitoring
B. Increase isolation
C. No collateral info
D. Independent detox
Answer: A

Vignette 196–200 — Social Anxiety Fear Scenario

Client: 23-year-old woman, avoids social events, fears humiliation, sweats/can't speak in groups, avoids job interviews.

196. Most likely diagnosis?
A. Social Anxiety Disorder
B. Agoraphobia
C. Paranoid Personality Disorder
D. Schizophrenia

Answer: A

197. First-line intervention?
A. Exposure + CBT for negative beliefs
B. Permanent avoidance
C. Medication only
D. Silence training
Answer: A

198. Assessment tool?
A. Liebowitz Social Anxiety Scale (LSAS)
B. CAGE
C. MoCA
D. Autism ADOS
Answer: A

199. Career impact focus?
A. Job interview role-play practice
B. Avoid interviewing
C. Shame client
D. Rely only on medication
Answer: A

200. Document impairments specifically in:
A. Social + occupational functioning
B. Fashion choices
C. Favorite music
D. Therapist's opinions
Answer: A

✅Batch 5 — Questions 201–250

CASE 201–210 — Adjustment, Medical Stressors, Ethics

Client Profile:
Angelica, 34, recently diagnosed with **multiple sclerosis**. Tearful, reporting fatigue, loss of independence, and relationship strain. No prior mental health history.

Q201. What is your **initial clinical priority**?
A. Explore childhood trauma
B. Assess current coping & functioning
C. Focus on medication side effects
D. Refer to neurologist for evaluation
✅ **Correct: B** — Determine present functioning to identify impairment.

Q202. Best *initial* diagnosis?
A. Major Depressive Disorder
B. Adjustment Disorder with Depressed Mood
C. Somatic Symptom Disorder
D. Illness Anxiety Disorder
✅ **Correct: B** — Symptoms tied directly to medical diagnosis and recent stressor.

Q203. Best evidence-based treatment?
A. EMDR
B. Acceptance and Commitment Therapy (ACT)
C. Prolonged Exposure
D. Confrontation of denial
✅ **Correct: B** — ACT is supported in chronic illness adaptation research.

Q204. Angelica discloses she sometimes wishes she were dead but denies plan/intent. Next?
A. Hospitalize immediately
B. Document and schedule 3-month follow-up
C. Conduct full suicide risk assessment
D. Ignore as part of grief
✅ **Correct: C** — Always assess further.

Q205. Ethical action when collaborating with neurologist?
A. Release all clinical notes automatically
B. Obtain informed consent for any information sharing
C. Share only if neurologist requests
D. HIPAA prevents any sharing
✅ **Correct: B**

Q206. A culturally responsive intervention?
A. Emphasize independence values
B. Encourage traditional support roles assigned to women
C. Explore cultural beliefs about disability
D. Avoid discussing culture
✅ **Correct: C**

Q207. Progress tracking measure?
A. MMSE
B. GAD-2
C. FIM (Functional Independence Measure) + PHQ-9
D. Rorschach
✅ **Correct: C**

Q208. If symptoms persist > 6 months and worsen:
A. PTSD
B. Persistent Depressive Disorder
C. Adjustment Disorder (still)
D. MDD
✅ **Correct: D** — Adjustment Disorder **cannot** exceed 6 months once stressor resolves.

Q209. Angelica asks you to write a letter exaggerating disability to support financial benefits. Ethical decision?
A. Do it to support client
B. Decline and discuss advocacy alternatives
C. Write but keep separate notes
D. Discharge client
✅ **Correct: B**

Q210. Best case management addition?
A. Nutrition counselor
B. MS support group referral
C. Anger management course
D. Couples therapy only
✅ **Correct: B**

CASE 211–220 — Bipolar vs. Substance Impact, Safety

Client Profile:
Desmond, 29 — brought by police after disorderly conduct. Grandiose, awake for 48 hrs, recently using cocaine. States he's "invincible." PHQ-9 = low. No SI/HI.

Q211. Highest-priority differential?
A. ADHD
B. Bipolar I vs. stimulant-induced mania
C. Persistent Depressive Disorder
D. Schizoaffective Disorder
✅ **Correct: B**

Q212. First action?
A. Do nothing
B. Immediate substance use assessment + safety check
C. Start couples counseling
D. Refer to life coach
✅ **Correct: B**

Q213. Family reports past similar episode **without** substances. Diagnosis?
A. Bipolar I, current manic episode
B. Substance-Induced Bipolar
C. Delusional Disorder
D. Panic Disorder
✅ **Correct: A**

Q214. Risk status?
A. Low
B. Moderate
C. High
D. Imminent
✅ **Correct: B** — Poor judgment & impulsivity elevate risk.

Q215. Intervention priority?
A. Sleep stabilization
B. Psychoanalysis

C. Journaling
D. Couples therapy
✅ **Correct: A**

Q216. Medication collaboration ethically requires?
A. Diagnose only after medication
B. Informed consent for release to psychiatrist
C. Share everything immediately
D. Refuse collaboration
✅ **Correct: B**

Q217. Best referral?
A. Massage therapy
B. Partial hospitalization or intensive outpatient program
C. General therapy monthly
D. Court-mandated anger class
✅ **Correct: B**

Q218. Long-term therapy approach?
A. DBT + relapse prevention
B. Play therapy
C. CBT-E
D. EMDR
✅ **Correct: A**

Q219. Worst action?
A. Involving support network
B. Reinforcing grandiosity
C. Sleep hygiene education
D. Crisis plan
✅ **Correct: B**

Q220. Monitoring tool?
A. Young Mania Rating Scale (YMRS)
B. AUDIT-C only
C. GAD-7 only
D. MMPI-A
✅ **Correct: A**

CASE 221–230 — Child Safety, Trauma, Systems Work

Client Profile:
Layla, 9. School counselor reports bruises. Client says dad "gets mad." Appears fearful, avoids eye contact.

Q221. Immediate priority?
A. Family therapy
B. Conduct mandated report
C. Teach coping skills
D. Explore if she deserved punishment
✅ **Correct: B** — Child safety = **always first**.

Q222. Appropriate first communication after report?
A. Ask police outcome
B. Notify parents immediately
C. Continue supportive rapport building
D. Disclose confidential details to teacher
✅ **Correct: C**

Q223. Likely diagnosis?
A. Conduct Disorder
B. PTSD (provisional)
C. DMDD
D. Autism Spectrum Disorder
✅ **Correct: B**

Q224. Trauma treatment for children?
A. TF-CBT
B. Exposure flooding
C. Rational Emotive Therapy
D. Couples therapy
✅ **Correct: A**

Q225. Safety planning includes:
A. Avoid social workers
B. Identify safe adults & emergency call list
C. Tell child to protect herself physically
D. Encourage secret-keeping

✅**Correct: B**

Q226. Mandated reporter rule?
A. Only report if proven
B. Report **suspected** abuse
C. Wait to see if improvements occur
D. Let school decide
✅**Correct: B**

Q227. Family expresses anger after report. Best response?
A. Apologize for reporting
B. Explain legal & ethical duty
C. Stop treatment
D. Minimize danger
✅**Correct: B**

Q228. Progress measure?
A. PHQ-9
B. Trauma Symptom Checklist for Children (TSCC)
C. YMRS
D. DAST-10
✅**Correct: B**

Q229. Primary treatment goal?
A. Reunify immediately
B. Increase distress tolerance + reduce hyperarousal
C. Teach career readiness
D. Assign punishments
✅**Correct: B**

Q230. Worst action?
A. Normalizing fear
B. Working with CPS collaboratively
C. Providing stability
D. Empowering voice
✅**Correct: A**

CASE 231–240 — Grief Complications vs. MDD

Client Profile:
Richard, 58 — wife died 3 months ago. PHQ-9: 18 (moderately severe). Suicidal thoughts about "wanting to join her," **no plan**. Neglecting hygiene. Denies medical issues.

Q231. Immediate focus?
A. Conduct lethality assessment
B. Interpret dreams
C. Encourage dating
D. Focus on childhood
✅ **Correct: A**

Q232. Best diagnosis?
A. Prolonged Grief Disorder
B. MDD — Single Episode, Severe
C. Persistent Complex Bereavement Disorder
D. Adjustment Disorder
✅ **Correct: B** — Significant functional impairment + suicidal ideation.

Q233. Best treatment modality?
A. Complicated grief treatment
B. Behavioral activation + CBT-D
C. Hypnosis
D. Psychoanalytic focus exclusively
✅ **Correct: B**

Q234. Supportive resource?
A. Hospice bereavement group
B. Anger management class
C. Parenting class
D. EMDR
✅ **Correct: A**

Q235. Ethical documentation?
A. Omit SI statements
B. Record safety plan + risk level

C. Vague charting to avoid liability
D. Avoid writing interventions
✅ **Correct: B**

Q236. Safety step?
A. Means restriction planning
B. Never ask details
C. Assume low risk
D. Wait until symptoms worsen
✅ **Correct: A**

Q237. A sign grief is normal?
A. Auditory hallucinations of spouse regularly
B. Decreased activities but maintaining hygiene
C. Unable to function at work
D. Prolonged detachment
✅ **Correct: B**

Q238. Best measure to track improvement?
A. ASRS
B. PHQ-9
C. Y-BOCS
D. CAPS-5
✅ **Correct: B**

Q239. Cultural sensitivity example?
A. Explore spiritual beliefs regarding mourning
B. Avoid cultural questions
C. Focus only on Western grief stages
D. Correct “irrational” mourning rituals
✅ **Correct: A**

Q240. Worst action?
A. Increase session frequency
B. Validate pain
C. Insist “you should move on”
D. Coordinate medication consult
✅ **Correct: C**

CASE 241–250 — Personality, Boundaries, Countertransference

Client Profile:
Serena, 31 — intense relationships, fear of abandonment, self-harm history (last episode 4 months ago). Splitting: "You're the only one who gets me." No SI today.

Q241. Most probable diagnosis?
A. Borderline Personality Disorder
B. Antisocial Personality Disorder
C. Bipolar II
D. Histrionic Personality Disorder
✅ **Correct: A**

Q242. Primary intervention approach?
A. DBT
B. Exposure therapy
C. Gestalt confrontation
D. Interpret defense mechanisms only
✅ **Correct: A**

Q243. Risk level?
A. Low
B. Moderate
C. High
D. Imminent
✅ **Correct: B** — self-harm history + emotional intensity.

Q244. First treatment goal?
A. Develop a trauma narrative
B. Crisis & emotion regulation skills
C. Terminate therapy
D. Focus only on insight
✅ **Correct: B**

Q245. Boundaries example?
A. Offering sessions at home
B. Strict session structure + clarity

C. Text relationship advice 24/7
D. Agree to "friendship" outside therapy
✅ **Correct: B**

Q246. When Serena threatens to quit after boundary setting:
A. Fearfully retract boundary
B. Maintain boundaries + validate feelings
C. Ignore threat
D. Terminate immediately
✅ **Correct: B**

Q247. Countertransference management?
A. Consultation + supervision
B. Suppress feelings silently
C. Act out irritation
D. Self-disclose deeply
✅ **Correct: A**

Q248. Progress tracking?
A. OQ-45 or DBT Diary Cards
B. YMRS
C. TOVA
D. ASRS
✅ **Correct: A**

Q249. Avoid?
A. Safety plan
B. Black-and-white labeling of therapist
C. Skills training
D. Consistency
✅ **Correct: B**

Q250. Cultural humility includes:
A. Discussing identity factors shaping attachment patterns
B. Avoid culture—focus only on skills
C. Push Western relational norms
D. Over-pathologize coping rooted in culture
✅ **Correct: A**

✅Batch 6 — Questions 251–300

CASE 251–260 — Adult PTSD + Military History

Client: 35-year-old male veteran, recently discharged. Reports nightmares, hypervigilance, anger outbursts, avoidance of crowds, and alcohol use. PHQ-9 = 14, PCL-5 = 52.

Q251. Most likely diagnosis?
A. GAD
B. PTSD
C. Adjustment Disorder
D. Major Depression
✅**Answer: B** — Trauma-related hyperarousal, avoidance, intrusive memories.

Q252. First assessment focus?
A. Substance use + trauma symptom severity
B. Childhood development only
C. Cognitive testing
D. Physical exam only
✅**Answer: A**

Q253. Best initial intervention?
A. Trauma-Focused CBT or CPT
B. Psychoanalysis
C. Meditation only
D. Exposure flooding
✅**Answer: A**

Q254. Alcohol use role?
A. Risk factor for functional impairment + poor coping
B. Self-limiting
C. No relation
D. Protective mechanism
✅**Answer: A**

Q255. Safety concern?
A. Anger outbursts + access to firearms

B. Sleeping on couch
C. Driving carefully
D. Following diet
✅ **Answer: A**

Q256. Evidence-based pharmacologic support?
A. SSRIs (e.g., sertraline, paroxetine)
B. Benzodiazepines as first-line
C. Antipsychotics only
D. Stimulants
✅ **Answer: A**

Q257. Long-term coping skills?
A. Stress management + grounding techniques
B. Avoid triggers completely
C. Self-medicate with alcohol
D. Complete social isolation
✅ **Answer: A**

Q258. Best way to engage support system?
A. Involve family/friends in psychoeducation
B. Avoid discussing military experiences
C. Discourage social support
D. Only group therapy
✅ **Answer: A**

Q259. Documentation priority?
A. Trauma exposure, functional impairment, risk factors
B. Therapist opinion on politics
C. General observations only
D. None required
✅ **Answer: A**

Q260. Cultural consideration?
A. Military identity + veteran community norms
B. Ignore veteran status
C. Enforce civilian norms
D. Discourage peer support

✅ **Answer: A**

CASE 261–270 — Adolescent Depression & Self-Harm

Client: 16-year-old female. Recent drop in grades, social withdrawal, reports cutting "sometimes to feel something." Passive SI, no plan. PHQ-9 = 17.

Q261. Highest priority?
A. Suicide/self-harm risk assessment
B. Psychoeducation on grades
C. Peer group assignment
D. Ignore risk
✅ **Answer: A**

Q262. Most likely diagnosis?
A. Major Depressive Disorder
B. Bipolar II
C. GAD
D. Conduct Disorder
✅ **Answer: A**

Q263. Evidence-based therapy?
A. CBT + DBT skills for adolescents
B. Psychodynamic only
C. Hypnosis
D. Supportive counseling only
✅ **Answer: A**

Q264. School involvement approach?
A. Coordinate with school counselor with consent
B. Share full psychiatric notes without consent
C. Avoid school entirely
D. Punitive approach
✅ **Answer: A**

Q265. Family involvement?
A. Teach distress tolerance + communication
B. Minimize discussion

C. Assign blame
D. Avoid parent meetings
✅**Answer: A**

Q266. Best short-term goal?
A. Reduce cutting behavior + ensure safety
B. Academic excellence only
C. Ignore minor cuts
D. Immediate hospitalization regardless of risk
✅**Answer: A**

Q267. Documentation?
A. Risk assessment, plan, interventions
B. Therapist subjective judgment only
C. General notes without risk info
D. None
✅**Answer: A**

Q268. When is hospitalization warranted?
A. Active suicidal plan + means access
B. Minor depressive symptoms
C. Only for aggression
D. Not required ever
✅**Answer: A**

Q269. Cultural consideration?
A. Family beliefs about mental health + stigma
B. Ignore culture
C. Overrule beliefs
D. Assume standard norms
✅**Answer: A**

Q270. Measure progress?
A. PHQ-A + self-harm diaries
B. IQ testing
C. Y-BOCS
D. GAD-7 only
✅**Answer: A**

CASE 271–280 — Adult Anxiety + Panic Disorder

Client: 28-year-old male. Recurrent panic attacks in public spaces, anticipatory anxiety, avoids crowded areas. Dizziness, chest tightness reported. No prior medical cardiac issues.

Q271. Likely diagnosis?
A. Panic Disorder
B. Social Anxiety Disorder
C. GAD
D. Agoraphobia
✅ **Answer: A**

Q272. Rule-out step?
A. Cardiac evaluation to exclude medical causes
B. Ignore physical symptoms
C. Psychoanalysis first
D. MRI only
✅ **Answer: A**

Q273. Evidence-based therapy?
A. CBT with interoceptive exposure
B. Hypnosis
C. EMDR
D. Psychoanalytic only
✅ **Answer: A**

Q274. First-line medication option?
A. SSRIs
B. Benzodiazepines only
C. Antipsychotics
D. Stimulants
✅ **Answer: A**

Q275. Safety/education point?
A. Teach avoidance reduction + coping skills
B. Avoid all triggers indefinitely
C. Ignore symptoms
D. Rely only on meds

✅**Answer: A**

Q276. Functional impairment measure?
A. Sheehan Disability Scale (SDS)
B. MoCA
C. YMRS
D. TSCC
✅**Answer: A**

Q277. When client reports panic at work?
A. Use immediate grounding + cognitive reframing
B. Encourage leaving job
C. Punish avoidance
D. Avoid discussion
✅**Answer: A**

Q278. Family/collateral involvement?
A. Educate about panic & support avoidance reduction
B. Ignore family
C. Encourage coddling
D. Blame client
✅**Answer: A**

Q279. Short-term goal?
A. Reduce frequency/intensity of attacks
B. Cure panic in one session
C. Ignore panic triggers
D. Focus solely on breathing exercises
✅**Answer: A**

Q280. Documentation priority?
A. Trigger events, intensity, interventions, functional impairment
B. Only therapy notes without context
C. Therapist opinion only
D. None
✅**Answer: A**

CASE 281–290 — Older Adult Cognitive Decline

Client: 74-year-old female. Forgetful, misplaces objects, mild confusion. History of hypertension. MMSE = 25/30. Reports frustration, low mood.

Q281. Likely diagnosis?
A. Mild Neurocognitive Disorder (MCI)
B. Alzheimer's Disease
C. Major Depression
D. Delirium
✅ **Answer: A**

Q282. Assessment priority?
A. Cognitive battery + functional assessment
B. Ignore memory complaints
C. Immediate hospitalization
D. Only physical exam
✅ **Answer: A**

Q283. Intervention?
A. Cognitive remediation + memory strategies
B. Hypnosis
C. EMDR
D. Psychoanalysis only
✅ **Answer: A**

Q284. Safety concern?
A. Driving assessment + fall risk
B. Dietary preferences only
C. Ignore functional changes
D. Only medication adjustments
✅ **Answer: A**

Q285. Mood monitoring?
A. GDS-15 (Geriatric Depression Scale)
B. MMSE only
C. YMRS
D. PHQ-A

✅**Answer: A**

Q286. Family support?
A. Education + realistic planning
B. Encourage complete independence
C. Avoid discussing decline
D. Punitive approach
✅**Answer: A**

Q287. Medication referral?
A. Consider cholinesterase inhibitors if progressive
B. High-dose stimulants
C. Benzodiazepines
D. Antipsychotics immediately
✅**Answer: A**

Q288. Ethical consideration?
A. Ensure autonomy + safety balance
B. Ignore decision-making
C. Make all decisions yourself
D. Force hospitalization
✅**Answer: A**

Q289. Cultural consideration?
A. Explore family expectations + caregiving norms
B. Ignore culture
C. Apply standard interventions rigidly
D. Assume Western elder norms
✅**Answer: A**

Q290. Progress tracking?
A. MMSE + functional ADL/IADL measures
B. PHQ-A only
C. Y-BOCS
D. LSAS
✅**Answer: A**

CASE 291–300 — Complex PTSD + Comorbid Substance Use

Client: 32-year-old female. History of childhood abuse, intimate partner violence, alcohol use, insomnia, nightmares, hypervigilance. PHQ-9 = 16, PCL-5 = 55. Reports urge to drink "to sleep."

Q291. Highest-priority focus?
A. Safety + substance use + trauma stabilization
B. Career counseling
C. Diet plan
D. Ignore trauma history
✅**Answer: A**

Q292. Most likely diagnosis?
A. PTSD with comorbid Alcohol Use Disorder
B. MDD only
C. Borderline Personality Disorder only
D. GAD
✅**Answer: A**

Q293. First-line therapy?
A. Integrated trauma + substance intervention (Seeking Safety, CBT)
B. Psychoanalysis
C. EMDR exclusively
D. Family therapy only
✅**Answer: A**

Q294. Risk factor?
A. Relapse under stress
B. High social functioning
C. No family history
D. Access to therapy
✅**Answer: A**

Q295. Medication support?
A. SSRIs + adjunct if needed for insomnia or cravings

B. Benzodiazepines freely
C. Antipsychotics only
D. Stimulants
✅**Answer: A**

Q296. Short-term goal?
A. Reduce alcohol intake + stabilize mood
B. Avoid triggers completely
C. Stop therapy
D. Ignore cravings
✅**Answer: A**

Q297. Long-term goal?
A. Trauma processing + relapse prevention
B. Complete independence immediately
C. Remove support system
D. Only meditation
✅**Answer: A**

Q298. Ethical documentation?
A. Record risk, treatment plan, consent, interventions
B. Only subjective notes
C. Skip risk documentation
D. Only treatment plans
✅**Answer: A**

Q299. Cultural sensitivity?
A. Explore trauma meaning in client's cultural context
B. Avoid cultural discussion
C. Apply generic Western models
D. Assume client's values
✅**Answer: A**

Q300. Progress measurement?
A. AUDIT + PCL-5 + session tracking
B. MoCA only
C. YMRS
D. TSCC only

✅**Answer: A**

✅**Batch 6 — Questions 251–300**

CASE 251–260 — Adult PTSD + Military History

Client: 35-year-old male veteran, recently discharged. Reports nightmares, hypervigilance, anger outbursts, avoidance of crowds, and alcohol use. PHQ-9 = 14, PCL-5 = 52.

Q251. Most likely diagnosis?
A. GAD
B. PTSD
C. Adjustment Disorder
D. Major Depression
✅**Answer: B** — Trauma-related hyperarousal, avoidance, intrusive memories.

Q252. First assessment focus?
A. Substance use + trauma symptom severity
B. Childhood development only
C. Cognitive testing
D. Physical exam only
✅**Answer: A**

Q253. Best initial intervention?
A. Trauma-Focused CBT or CPT
B. Psychoanalysis
C. Meditation only
D. Exposure flooding
✅**Answer: A**

Q254. Alcohol use role?
A. Risk factor for functional impairment + poor coping
B. Self-limiting
C. No relation
D. Protective mechanism
✅**Answer: A**

Q255. Safety concern?
A. Anger outbursts + access to firearms
B. Sleeping on couch
C. Driving carefully
D. Following diet
✅**Answer: A**

Q256. Evidence-based pharmacologic support?
A. SSRIs (e.g., sertraline, paroxetine)
B. Benzodiazepines as first-line
C. Antipsychotics only
D. Stimulants
✅**Answer: A**

Q257. Long-term coping skills?
A. Stress management + grounding techniques
B. Avoid triggers completely
C. Self-medicate with alcohol
D. Complete social isolation
✅**Answer: A**

Q258. Best way to engage support system?
A. Involve family/friends in psychoeducation
B. Avoid discussing military experiences
C. Discourage social support
D. Only group therapy
✅**Answer: A**

Q259. Documentation priority?
A. Trauma exposure, functional impairment, risk factors
B. Therapist opinion on politics
C. General observations only
D. None required
✅**Answer: A**

Q260. Cultural consideration?
A. Military identity + veteran community norms
B. Ignore veteran status

C. Enforce civilian norms
D. Discourage peer support
✅**Answer: A**

CASE 261–270 — Adolescent Depression & Self-Harm

Client: 16-year-old female. Recent drop in grades, social withdrawal, reports cutting "sometimes to feel something." Passive SI, no plan. PHQ-9 = 17.

Q261. Highest priority?
A. Suicide/self-harm risk assessment
B. Psychoeducation on grades
C. Peer group assignment
D. Ignore risk
✅**Answer: A**

Q262. Most likely diagnosis?
A. Major Depressive Disorder
B. Bipolar II
C. GAD
D. Conduct Disorder
✅**Answer: A**

Q263. Evidence-based therapy?
A. CBT + DBT skills for adolescents
B. Psychodynamic only
C. Hypnosis
D. Supportive counseling only
✅**Answer: A**

Q264. School involvement approach?
A. Coordinate with school counselor with consent
B. Share full psychiatric notes without consent
C. Avoid school entirely
D. Punitive approach
✅**Answer: A**

Q265. Family involvement?

A. Teach distress tolerance + communication
B. Minimize discussion
C. Assign blame
D. Avoid parent meetings
✅ **Answer: A**

Q266. Best short-term goal?
A. Reduce cutting behavior + ensure safety
B. Academic excellence only
C. Ignore minor cuts
D. Immediate hospitalization regardless of risk
✅ **Answer: A**

Q267. Documentation?
A. Risk assessment, plan, interventions
B. Therapist subjective judgment only
C. General notes without risk info
D. None
✅ **Answer: A**

Q268. When is hospitalization warranted?
A. Active suicidal plan + means access
B. Minor depressive symptoms
C. Only for aggression
D. Not required ever
✅ **Answer: A**

Q269. Cultural consideration?
A. Family beliefs about mental health + stigma
B. Ignore culture
C. Overrule beliefs
D. Assume standard norms
✅ **Answer: A**

Q270. Measure progress?
A. PHQ-A + self-harm diaries
B. IQ testing
C. Y-BOCS

D. GAD-7 only
✅ **Answer: A**

CASE 271–280 — Adult Anxiety + Panic Disorder

Client: 28-year-old male. Recurrent panic attacks in public spaces, anticipatory anxiety, avoids crowded areas. Dizziness, chest tightness reported. No prior medical cardiac issues.

Q271. Likely diagnosis?
A. Panic Disorder
B. Social Anxiety Disorder
C. GAD
D. Agoraphobia
✅ **Answer: A**

Q272. Rule-out step?
A. Cardiac evaluation to exclude medical causes
B. Ignore physical symptoms
C. Psychoanalysis first
D. MRI only
✅ **Answer: A**

Q273. Evidence-based therapy?
A. CBT with interoceptive exposure
B. Hypnosis
C. EMDR
D. Psychoanalytic only
✅ **Answer: A**

Q274. First-line medication option?
A. SSRIs
B. Benzodiazepines only
C. Antipsychotics
D. Stimulants
✅ **Answer: A**

Q275. Safety/education point?
A. Teach avoidance reduction + coping skills

B. Avoid all triggers indefinitely
C. Ignore symptoms
D. Rely only on meds
✅ **Answer: A**

Q276. Functional impairment measure?
A. Sheehan Disability Scale (SDS)
B. MoCA
C. YMRS
D. TSCC
✅ **Answer: A**

Q277. When client reports panic at work?
A. Use immediate grounding + cognitive reframing
B. Encourage leaving job
C. Punish avoidance
D. Avoid discussion
✅ **Answer: A**

Q278. Family/collateral involvement?
A. Educate about panic & support avoidance reduction
B. Ignore family
C. Encourage coddling
D. Blame client
✅ **Answer: A**

Q279. Short-term goal?
A. Reduce frequency/intensity of attacks
B. Cure panic in one session
C. Ignore panic triggers
D. Focus solely on breathing exercises
✅ **Answer: A**

Q280. Documentation priority?
A. Trigger events, intensity, interventions, functional impairment
B. Only therapy notes without context
C. Therapist opinion only
D. None

✅**Answer: A**

CASE 281–290 — Older Adult Cognitive Decline

Client: 74-year-old female. Forgetful, misplaces objects, mild confusion. History of hypertension. MMSE = 25/30. Reports frustration, low mood.

Q281. Likely diagnosis?
A. Mild Neurocognitive Disorder (MCI)
B. Alzheimer's Disease
C. Major Depression
D. Delirium
✅**Answer: A**

Q282. Assessment priority?
A. Cognitive battery + functional assessment
B. Ignore memory complaints
C. Immediate hospitalization
D. Only physical exam
✅**Answer: A**

Q283. Intervention?
A. Cognitive remediation + memory strategies
B. Hypnosis
C. EMDR
D. Psychoanalysis only
✅**Answer: A**

Q284. Safety concern?
A. Driving assessment + fall risk
B. Dietary preferences only
C. Ignore functional changes
D. Only medication adjustments
✅**Answer: A**

Q285. Mood monitoring?
A. GDS-15 (Geriatric Depression Scale)
B. MMSE only

C. YMRS
D. PHQ-A
✅**Answer: A**

Q286. Family support?
A. Education + realistic planning
B. Encourage complete independence
C. Avoid discussing decline
D. Punitive approach
✅**Answer: A**

Q287. Medication referral?
A. Consider cholinesterase inhibitors if progressive
B. High-dose stimulants
C. Benzodiazepines
D. Antipsychotics immediately
✅**Answer: A**

Q288. Ethical consideration?
A. Ensure autonomy + safety balance
B. Ignore decision-making
C. Make all decisions yourself
D. Force hospitalization
✅**Answer: A**

Q289. Cultural consideration?
A. Explore family expectations + caregiving norms
B. Ignore culture
C. Apply standard interventions rigidly
D. Assume Western elder norms
✅**Answer: A**

Q290. Progress tracking?
A. MMSE + functional ADL/IADL measures
B. PHQ-A only
C. Y-BOCS
D. LSAS
✅**Answer: A**

CASE 291–300 — Complex PTSD + Comorbid Substance Use

Client: 32-year-old female. History of childhood abuse, intimate partner violence, alcohol use, insomnia, nightmares, hypervigilance. PHQ-9 = 16, PCL-5 = 55. Reports urge to drink "to sleep."

Q291. Highest-priority focus?
A. Safety + substance use + trauma stabilization
B. Career counseling
C. Diet plan
D. Ignore trauma history
✅ **Answer: A**

Q292. Most likely diagnosis?
A. PTSD with comorbid Alcohol Use Disorder
B. MDD only
C. Borderline Personality Disorder only
D. GAD
✅ **Answer: A**

Q293. First-line therapy?
A. Integrated trauma + substance intervention (Seeking Safety, CBT)
B. Psychoanalysis
C. EMDR exclusively
D. Family therapy only
✅ **Answer: A**

Q294. Risk factor?
A. Relapse under stress
B. High social functioning
C. No family history
D. Access to therapy
✅ **Answer: A**

Q295. Medication support?
A. SSRIs + adjunct if needed for insomnia or cravings

B. Benzodiazepines freely
C. Antipsychotics only
D. Stimulants
✅**Answer: A**

Q296. Short-term goal?
A. Reduce alcohol intake + stabilize mood
B. Avoid triggers completely
C. Stop therapy
D. Ignore cravings
✅**Answer: A**

Q297. Long-term goal?
A. Trauma processing + relapse prevention
B. Complete independence immediately
C. Remove support system
D. Only meditation
✅**Answer: A**

Q298. Ethical documentation?
A. Record risk, treatment plan, consent, interventions
B. Only subjective notes
C. Skip risk documentation
D. Only treatment plans
✅**Answer: A**

Q299. Cultural sensitivity?
A. Explore trauma meaning in client's cultural context
B. Avoid cultural discussion
C. Apply generic Western models
D. Assume client's values
✅**Answer: A**

Q300. Progress measurement?
A. AUDIT + PCL-5 + session tracking
B. MoCA only
C. YMRS
D. TSCC only

✅**Answer: A**

✅**Batch 6 complete — Questions 251–300 done.**
We now have **300/999 questions** — nearly a third completed. ?

Next step options:

A) Continue **Batch 7: 301–350**
B) Start creating a **combined .docx with Batches 1–6**
C) Begin **adding detailed rationales** for each answer

Reply: **A**, **B**, or **C**

Vous avez dit :

Continue Batch 7: 301–350

Absolutely! Let's keep the momentum going ?
Here is **Batch 7: Questions 301–350**, NCMHCE-style, vignette-based, with DSM-5-TR alignment, interventions, risk/ethics, and functional assessment notes.

✅**Batch 7 — Questions 301–350**

CASE 301–310 — Adult OCD + Functional Impairment

Client: 28-year-old female. Reports intrusive thoughts about contamination, repetitive handwashing (up to 3 hrs/day), avoidance of public spaces. PHQ-9 = 12, Y-BOCS = 28.

Q301. Most likely diagnosis?
A. GAD
B. OCD
C. Panic Disorder
D. Social Anxiety Disorder
✅**Answer: B**

Q302. First-line intervention?
A. Exposure and Response Prevention (ERP)
B. Psychoanalysis

C. Hypnosis
D. General supportive therapy
✅ **Answer: A**

Q303. Medication support?
A. SSRIs at therapeutic doses
B. Benzodiazepines alone
C. Antipsychotics monotherapy
D. Stimulants
✅ **Answer: A**

Q304. Safety/functional risk?
A. Skin damage, infection, social isolation
B. Only mental focus
C. Academic risk is irrelevant
D. No risk present
✅ **Answer: A**

Q305. Progress measure?
A. Yale-Brown Obsessive Compulsive Scale (Y-BOCS)
B. PHQ-A only
C. MoCA
D. LSAS
✅ **Answer: A**

Q306. Secondary concern?
A. Depression due to functional impairment
B. Substance abuse
C. Bipolar disorder
D. Schizophrenia
✅ **Answer: A**

Q307. Short-term treatment goal?
A. Reduce compulsive behaviors by 25–50%
B. Complete elimination immediately
C. Ignore behaviors
D. Focus only on intrusive thoughts
✅ **Answer: A**

Q308. Ethical documentation?
A. Record symptoms, interventions, consent, and functional impact
B. Only therapist impressions
C. Skip Y-BOCS
D. General notes
✅ **Answer: A**

Q309. When client avoids ERP?
A. Use motivational interviewing + graded exposure
B. Punish non-compliance
C. Ignore avoidance
D. Terminate therapy
✅ **Answer: A**

Q310. Family/collateral involvement?
A. Psychoeducation + avoidance management
B. Avoid family entirely
C. Assign blame to family
D. Encourage enmeshment
✅ **Answer: A**

CASE 311–320 — Adolescent Anxiety & Academic Stress

Client: 17-year-old male. Severe test anxiety, sleep disruption, panic episodes before exams. Avoids extracurricular activities. PHQ-9 = 10, GAD-7 = 15.

Q311. Most likely diagnosis?
A. GAD
B. Panic Disorder
C. OCD
D. Social Anxiety Disorder
✅ **Answer: A**

Q312. Immediate intervention?
A. CBT for anxiety + coping skills
B. Hypnosis

C. EMDR
D. Psychoanalysis
✅ **Answer: A**

Q313. School coordination?
A. Collaborate with counselor for accommodations
B. Avoid school involvement
C. Punitive measures
D. Ignore academic stress
✅ **Answer: A**

Q314. Short-term goal?
A. Reduce panic episodes, improve sleep
B. Eliminate all anxiety immediately
C. Ignore test performance
D. Increase study load
✅ **Answer: A**

Q315. Risk monitoring?
A. SI/HI, functional impairment
B. IQ testing only
C. Attendance only
D. Physical exam
✅ **Answer: A**

Q316. Evidence-based adjunct intervention?
A. Relaxation training, breathing exercises
B. Avoid exposure
C. Confrontational techniques
D. Isolation
✅ **Answer: A**

Q317. Long-term goal?
A. Build resilience + anxiety management skills
B. Remove academic responsibilities
C. Social withdrawal encouraged
D. Only meditation
✅ **Answer: A**

Q318. Ethical consideration?
A. Consent for school collaboration
B. Share grades publicly
C. Punish absenteeism
D. Avoid adolescent voice
✅ **Answer: A**

Q319. Cultural sensitivity?
A. Explore family expectations and academic pressure norms
B. Apply generic interventions
C. Ignore cultural context
D. Assume Western academic standards
✅ **Answer: A**

Q320. Progress tracking?
A. GAD-7 + panic episode logs
B. MMSE
C. MoCA
D. LSAS
✅ **Answer: A**

CASE 321–330 — Adult Bipolar II + Relationship Stress

Client: 32-year-old male. Mood swings (2 weeks depression, 3 days hypomania), irritability, sleep disruption. Reports conflict with spouse. PHQ-9 = 16, YMRS = 10.

Q321. Likely diagnosis?
A. Bipolar II
B. MDD
C. Cyclothymia
D. Borderline Personality
✅ **Answer: A**

Q322. First step?
A. Assess mood episode patterns + functional impairment
B. Focus only on relationship conflict
C. Ignore hypomanic symptoms

D. Psychoanalysis
✅**Answer: A**

Q323. Evidence-based intervention?
A. CBT for bipolar disorder + mood monitoring
B. Hypnosis
C. Play therapy
D. EMDR only
✅**Answer: A**

Q324. Medication consultation?
A. Mood stabilizer coordination with psychiatrist
B. Prescribe SSRI independently
C. Avoid medications
D. Start benzodiazepines long-term
✅**Answer: A**

Q325. Family involvement?
A. Psychoeducation on mood recognition + stress reduction
B. Exclude spouse
C. Ignore marital conflict
D. Punitive strategies
✅**Answer: A**

Q326. Short-term goal?
A. Stabilize sleep + mood patterns
B. Eliminate mood swings immediately
C. Ignore irritability
D. Confront spouse aggressively
✅**Answer: A**

Q327. Risk monitoring?
A. Suicide, impulsivity, relational conflict
B. Academic testing only
C. Ignore past episodes
D. Physical fitness
✅**Answer: A**

Q328. Long-term goal?

A. Relapse prevention + coping strategies
B. Avoid social interactions
C. Terminate therapy prematurely
D. Ignore sleep hygiene
✅ **Answer: A**

Q329. Documentation focus?
A. Mood charting, interventions, functional impact
B. Therapist subjective opinion only
C. Ignore hypomanic episodes
D. General notes
✅ **Answer: A**

Q330. Cultural consideration?
A. Consider cultural norms around emotional expression and family roles
B. Apply only Western norms
C. Ignore context
D. Force conformity
✅ **Answer: A**

CASE 331–340 — Adult Substance Use + Depression

Client: 40-year-old female. Daily alcohol use (4–5 drinks), low mood, difficulty maintaining job, isolates socially. PHQ-9 = 18, AUDIT = 24.

Q331. Likely diagnosis?
A. MDD + Alcohol Use Disorder
B. GAD
C. Bipolar II
D. Panic Disorder
✅ **Answer: A**

Q332. First priority?
A. Safety + substance reduction + functional assessment
B. Psychoanalysis
C. Ignore drinking

D. Focus only on depression
✅**Answer: A**

Q333. Evidence-based intervention?
A. Integrated CBT for depression + substance use
B. EMDR only
C. Supportive therapy alone
D. Hypnosis exclusively
✅**Answer: A**

Q334. Short-term goal?
A. Reduce drinking + improve daily functioning
B. Immediate abstinence without support
C. Ignore job issues
D. Avoid family involvement
✅**Answer: A**

Q335. Risk assessment includes?
A. Suicide, relapse triggers, medical consequences
B. Only mood
C. Only substance quantity
D. None
✅**Answer: A**

Q336. Medication support?
A. SSRIs for depression, adjunct if needed
B. Benzodiazepines freely
C. Stimulants
D. Antipsychotics only
✅**Answer: A**

Q337. Family/collateral involvement?
A. Psychoeducation + support in recovery plan
B. Ignore family
C. Enable drinking
D. Punish client
✅**Answer: A**

Q338. Documentation priority?

A. Symptoms, interventions, consent, functional impairment
B. Subjective notes only
C. Ignore drinking data
D. Only treatment plan
✅ **Answer: A**

Q339. Cultural sensitivity?
A. Assess cultural norms around alcohol, stigma, and support networks
B. Ignore culture
C. Apply generic interventions
D. Assume all norms are same
✅ **Answer: A**

Q340. Progress tracking?
A. PHQ-9 + AUDIT + daily logs
B. MoCA only
C. LSAS
D. YMRS
✅ **Answer: A**

CASE 341–350 — Older Adult Anxiety + Chronic Illness

Client: 68-year-old male. Type 2 Diabetes, chronic pain. Reports excessive worry about health, sleep disturbance, poor appetite, and mild depressive symptoms. PHQ-9 = 12, GAD-7 = 14.

Q341. Likely diagnosis?
A. GAD
B. MDD
C. Panic Disorder
D. Adjustment Disorder
✅ **Answer: A**

Q342. First assessment focus?
A. Functional impairment, anxiety triggers, medical status
B. Ignore physical conditions

C. Only mood assessment
D. IQ test
✅**Answer: A**

Q343. Evidence-based therapy?
A. CBT for GAD + relaxation training
B. Psychoanalysis only
C. EMDR
D. Hypnosis only
✅**Answer: A**

Q344. Medication support?
A. SSRIs if indicated, monitor for medical interactions
B. Benzodiazepines long-term
C. Stimulants
D. Antipsychotics
✅**Answer: A**

Q345. Short-term goal?
A. Reduce worry + improve sleep
B. Cure chronic illness
C. Avoid medical adherence
D. Social isolation encouraged
✅**Answer: A**

Q346. Family/collateral involvement?
A. Education on illness management + anxiety support
B. Avoid family
C. Ignore caregiving context
D. Punitive approach
✅**Answer: A**

Q347. Risk monitoring?
A. Falls, medication adherence, SI
B. IQ only
C. Cognitive testing irrelevant
D. None
✅**Answer: A**

Q348. Documentation priority?
A. Symptoms, interventions, functional impact, safety
B. Therapist opinion only
C. Ignore physical conditions
D. General notes
✅**Answer: A**

Q349. Cultural sensitivity?
A. Explore beliefs about aging, illness, and family support
B. Ignore culture
C. Apply only Western norms
D. Force compliance
✅**Answer: A**

Q350. Progress tracking?
A. GAD-7 + sleep logs + functional ADL measures
B. PHQ-A only
C. YMRS
D. LSAS
✅**Answer: A**

✅Batch 8 — Questions 351–400

CASE 351–360 — Adult Major Depression + Chronic Pain

Client: 45-year-old male. Reports chronic lower back pain, low mood, fatigue, loss of interest in activities, poor appetite. PHQ-9 = 20. Pain impairs work.

Q351. Most likely diagnosis?
A. Major Depressive Disorder (MDD)
B. Adjustment Disorder
C. GAD
D. Bipolar II
✅**Answer: A**

Q352. Initial assessment focus?
A. Functional impairment, pain severity, depressive symptoms

B. Only mood
C. Only medical conditions
D. IQ test
✅**Answer: A**

Q353. Evidence-based therapy?
A. CBT + behavioral activation tailored to chronic pain
B. Psychoanalysis
C. EMDR
D. Hypnosis only
✅**Answer: A**

Q354. Medication support?
A. SSRIs, consider adjunct pain management
B. Benzodiazepines alone
C. Antipsychotics
D. Stimulants
✅**Answer: A**

Q355. Short-term goal?
A. Improve mood, increase daily activity, reduce functional impairment
B. Cure pain completely immediately
C. Ignore work impairment
D. Avoid daily routines
✅**Answer: A**

Q356. Risk monitoring?
A. Suicidal ideation, chronic pain exacerbation, functional loss
B. IQ only
C. Ignore suicidal thoughts
D. Only physical assessment
✅**Answer: A**

Q357. Family/collateral involvement?
A. Psychoeducation about depression + pain coping
B. Avoid family
C. Punitive approaches

D. Ignore relational context
✅ **Answer: A**

Q358. Ethical documentation?
A. Record depressive symptoms, interventions, functional impact, consent
B. Subjective impressions only
C. Skip risk notes
D. General notes only
✅ **Answer: A**

Q359. Cultural consideration?
A. Explore beliefs about pain, mental health stigma, and coping norms
B. Ignore cultural context
C. Force standard Western approaches
D. Apply generic interventions
✅ **Answer: A**

Q360. Progress tracking?
A. PHQ-9 + pain diary + functional activity logs
B. MoCA only
C. LSAS
D. YMRS
✅ **Answer: A**

CASE 361–370 — Adolescent Substance Use + Depression

Client: 16-year-old male. Reports daily vaping and alcohol use, withdrawal from friends, low motivation. PHQ-9 = 15, CRAFFT = 3.

Q361. Likely diagnosis?
A. MDD + Substance Use Disorder
B. ADHD
C. Conduct Disorder only
D. GAD
✅ **Answer: A**

Q362. Initial priority?
A. Safety, substance assessment, mood evaluation
B. Ignore substance use
C. Academic performance only
D. Psychoanalysis only
✅**Answer: A**

Q363. Evidence-based therapy?
A. Integrated CBT for depression + substance use (e.g., Motivational Interviewing)
B. EMDR
C. Hypnosis
D. Supportive counseling only
✅**Answer: A**

Q364. Short-term goal?
A. Reduce substance use + improve daily functioning
B. Complete abstinence immediately without support
C. Ignore social withdrawal
D. Focus only on academics
✅**Answer: A**

Q365. Risk assessment?
A. Suicide, impulsivity, relapse triggers
B. IQ only
C. Attendance only
D. Ignore risk
✅**Answer: A**

Q366. Family/collateral involvement?
A. Parent psychoeducation + support for behavior monitoring
B. Avoid family
C. Punish adolescent
D. Enable substance use
✅**Answer: A**

Q367. Ethical consideration?
A. Obtain consent for family involvement and school

communication
B. Share info freely
C. Avoid documentation
D. Ignore parental concerns
✅ **Answer: A**

Q368. Cultural sensitivity?
A. Consider family beliefs about substance use, mental health stigma
B. Ignore culture
C. Apply generic interventions
D. Force compliance
✅ **Answer: A**

Q369. Progress tracking?
A. PHQ-9 + CRAFFT + weekly logs
B. MoCA only
C. YMRS
D. LSAS
✅ **Answer: A**

Q370. Long-term goal?
A. Maintain sobriety + manage depressive symptoms + social reintegration
B. Avoid friends indefinitely
C. Ignore mood symptoms
D. Only focus on academics
✅ **Answer: A**

CASE 371–380 — Adult Anxiety + Workplace Stress

Client: 38-year-old female. Reports excessive worry about work performance, insomnia, irritability, headaches. GAD-7 = 16, PHQ-9 = 10.

Q371. Likely diagnosis?
A. GAD
B. Panic Disorder

C. OCD
D. MDD
✅**Answer: A**

Q372. First assessment?
A. Functional impairment, triggers, stress management
B. Ignore workplace context
C. Only mood
D. IQ test
✅**Answer: A**

Q373. Evidence-based therapy?
A. CBT for GAD + relaxation training + problem-solving skills
B. Psychoanalysis
C. EMDR
D. Hypnosis only
✅**Answer: A**

Q374. Short-term goal?
A. Reduce worry + improve sleep + manage headaches
B. Cure anxiety immediately
C. Avoid workplace
D. Ignore triggers
✅**Answer: A**

Q375. Medication support?
A. SSRIs if indicated
B. Benzodiazepines long-term
C. Stimulants
D. Antipsychotics
✅**Answer: A**

Q376. Risk monitoring?
A. Functional impairment, SI, somatic complaints
B. IQ only
C. Attendance only
D. None
✅**Answer: A**

Q377. Family/collateral involvement?
A. Psychoeducation on stress + support strategies
B. Avoid family
C. Punitive strategies
D. Ignore social support
✅**Answer: A**

Q378. Cultural consideration?
A. Explore cultural norms around work, stress, and coping
B. Ignore culture
C. Force standard approaches
D. Apply generic interventions
✅**Answer: A**

Q379. Documentation priority?
A. Symptoms, interventions, functional impact, consent
B. Therapist opinion only
C. Ignore stressors
D. General notes only
✅**Answer: A**

Q380. Progress tracking?
A. GAD-7 + sleep logs + headache tracking
B. MoCA only
C. LSAS
D. YMRS
✅**Answer: A**

CASE 381–390 — Older Adult Cognitive + Mood Concerns

Client: 72-year-old male. Mild memory lapses, occasional confusion, low mood, difficulty managing finances. MMSE = 26, PHQ-9 = 14.

Q381. Likely diagnosis?
A. Mild Neurocognitive Disorder + Depression
B. Alzheimer's Disease only
C. GAD

D. Panic Disorder
✅**Answer: A**

Q382. Assessment focus?
A. Cognitive function, ADLs/IADLs, mood, safety
B. Ignore mood
C. Only memory testing
D. IQ only
✅**Answer: A**

Q383. Short-term goal?
A. Improve coping strategies + daily functioning + mood
B. Cure cognitive decline immediately
C. Avoid daily tasks
D. Ignore depressive symptoms
✅**Answer: A**

Q384. Evidence-based therapy?
A. Cognitive remediation + CBT for depression + compensatory strategies
B. Psychoanalysis only
C. EMDR
D. Hypnosis only
✅**Answer: A**

Q385. Risk monitoring?
A. Falls, medication adherence, functional impairment
B. IQ only
C. Cognitive testing irrelevant
D. None
✅**Answer: A**

Q386. Family/collateral involvement?
A. Education + support for ADLs, safety planning
B. Avoid family
C. Punitive strategies
D. Ignore caregiving context
✅**Answer: A**

Q387. Medication support?
A. SSRIs for depression if indicated
B. Benzodiazepines long-term
C. Stimulants
D. Antipsychotics only
✅**Answer: A**

Q388. Ethical consideration?
A. Ensure autonomy + safety balance
B. Ignore decision-making
C. Force hospitalization
D. Make all decisions independently
✅**Answer: A**

Q389. Cultural sensitivity?
A. Explore beliefs about aging, illness, and family support
B. Ignore culture
C. Force Western norms
D. Apply generic interventions
✅**Answer: A**

Q390. Progress tracking?
A. MMSE + functional ADL/IADL measures + PHQ-9
B. LSAS only
C. YMRS
D. MoCA only
✅**Answer: A**

CASE 391–400 — Adult Trauma + Substance Use

Client: 30-year-old female. Reports childhood abuse, intimate partner trauma, current alcohol use, nightmares, hypervigilance. PHQ-9 = 17, PCL-5 = 54, AUDIT = 20.

Q391. Highest-priority focus?
A. Safety + trauma stabilization + substance use
B. Career counseling
C. Diet plan

D. Ignore trauma history
✅**Answer: A**

Q392. Likely diagnosis?
A. PTSD + Alcohol Use Disorder
B. MDD only
C. Bipolar II only
D. GAD only
✅**Answer: A**

Q393. Evidence-based therapy?
A. Integrated trauma + substance intervention (Seeking Safety, CBT)
B. Psychoanalysis
C. EMDR exclusively
D. Family therapy only
✅**Answer: A**

Q394. Short-term goal?
A. Reduce alcohol use + stabilize mood + reduce trauma symptoms
B. Immediate abstinence without support
C. Ignore cravings
D. Avoid therapy
✅**Answer: A**

Q395. Long-term goal?
A. Trauma processing + relapse prevention
B. Social withdrawal
C. Avoid emotional processing
D. Only meditation
✅**Answer: A**

Q396. Risk monitoring?
A. Suicide, relapse, interpersonal safety
B. IQ only
C. Attendance only
D. Ignore risk

✅**Answer: A**

Q397. Medication support?
A. SSRIs for PTSD/depression + adjunct for cravings if needed
B. Benzodiazepines freely
C. Antipsychotics only
D. Stimulants
✅**Answer: A**

Q398. Family/collateral involvement?
A. Psychoeducation + support network involvement
B. Ignore family
C. Enable substance use
D. Punitive approach
✅**Answer: A**

Q399. Cultural consideration?
A. Explore trauma meaning in client's cultural context
B. Ignore culture
C. Apply generic Western interventions
D. Assume client's values
✅**Answer: A**

Q400. Progress tracking?
A. AUDIT + PCL-5 + session tracking + functional assessment
B. MoCA only
C. YMRS
D. TSCC only
✅**Answer: A**

✅Batch 9 — Questions 401–450

CASE 401–410 — Adult PTSD + Relationship Conflict

Client: 34-year-old male. Reports intrusive memories of past assault, nightmares, irritability, difficulty trusting partner, avoidance of social situations. PHQ-9 = 15, PCL-5 = 56.

Q401. Likely diagnosis?

A. PTSD
B. GAD
C. Adjustment Disorder
D. MDD
✅ **Answer: A**

Q402. Initial assessment focus?
A. Trauma history, functional impact, safety
B. Only partner conflict
C. Childhood only
D. IQ test
✅ **Answer: A**

Q403. Evidence-based therapy?
A. Trauma-Focused CBT or CPT
B. Psychoanalysis only
C. Hypnosis
D. Supportive therapy exclusively
✅ **Answer: A**

Q404. Short-term goal?
A. Reduce nightmares + intrusive thoughts + improve relational trust
B. Eliminate trauma memories immediately
C. Avoid partner entirely
D. Focus only on anger
✅ **Answer: A**

Q405. Risk monitoring?
A. Aggression, SI, relationship dysfunction
B. Only depression
C. Ignore functional impairment
D. IQ testing
✅ **Answer: A**

Q406. Medication support?
A. SSRIs (sertraline, paroxetine)
B. Benzodiazepines first-line

C. Antipsychotics only
D. Stimulants
✅**Answer: A**

Q407. Family/collateral involvement?
A. Partner education + safe communication strategies
B. Avoid partner
C. Assign blame
D. Enmeshment
✅**Answer: A**

Q408. Documentation priority?
A. Trauma details, interventions, functional impairment, risk
B. Subjective notes only
C. Ignore partner conflict
D. General notes
✅**Answer: A**

Q409. Cultural consideration?
A. Military, ethnic, or social norms around trauma disclosure
B. Ignore culture
C. Force Western norms
D. Apply generic interventions
✅**Answer: A**

Q410. Progress tracking?
A. PCL-5 + sleep logs + functional assessments
B. PHQ-A only
C. MoCA
D. LSAS
✅**Answer: A**

CASE 411–420 — Adolescent Depression + Self-Harm

Client: 15-year-old female. Reports social withdrawal, cutting episodes, low mood, hopelessness. PHQ-9 = 18. Passive SI, no plan.

Q411. Highest-priority focus?

A. Suicide/self-harm risk assessment
B. Academic performance
C. Peer socialization only
D. Ignore risk
✅ **Answer: A**

Q412. Likely diagnosis?
A. Major Depressive Disorder
B. Bipolar II
C. GAD
D. Adjustment Disorder
✅ **Answer: A**

Q413. Evidence-based therapy?
A. CBT + DBT skills for adolescents
B. Psychoanalysis
C. Hypnosis only
D. Supportive counseling exclusively
✅ **Answer: A**

Q414. Short-term goal?
A. Reduce self-harm + stabilize mood
B. Immediate elimination of all symptoms
C. Ignore cutting
D. Focus only on academics
✅ **Answer: A**

Q415. Risk assessment includes?
A. SI/HI, functional impairment, triggers
B. IQ only
C. Attendance only
D. Physical exam only
✅ **Answer: A**

Q416. Family involvement?
A. Teach communication, emotional regulation, and safety planning
B. Avoid family

C. Assign blame
D. Ignore relational context
✅**Answer: A**

Q417. School coordination?
A. Collaborate with school counselor with consent
B. Share all details without consent
C. Avoid school entirely
D. Punitive measures
✅**Answer: A**

Q418. Documentation priority?
A. Risk assessment, interventions, functional impact, consent
B. Therapist opinion only
C. Ignore cutting or SI
D. General notes
✅**Answer: A**

Q419. Cultural consideration?
A. Family beliefs about mental health, stigma, coping norms
B. Ignore culture
C. Apply generic interventions
D. Force compliance
✅**Answer: A**

Q420. Progress tracking?
A. PHQ-9 + self-harm diary + functional monitoring
B. MoCA only
C. YMRS
D. LSAS
✅**Answer: A**

CASE 421–430 — Adult Panic Disorder + Agoraphobia

Client: 30-year-old male. Panic attacks in crowds, dizziness, chest tightness, avoidance of public spaces. No cardiac history.

Q421. Likely diagnosis?
A. Panic Disorder

B. GAD
C. Social Anxiety Disorder
D. OCD
✅ **Answer: A**

Q422. Rule-out step?
A. Cardiac evaluation
B. Ignore physical symptoms
C. MRI only
D. Psychoanalysis first
✅ **Answer: A**

Q423. Evidence-based therapy?
A. CBT with interoceptive exposure
B. Hypnosis
C. Psychoanalysis
D. EMDR only
✅ **Answer: A**

Q424. Medication support?
A. SSRIs
B. Benzodiazepines alone
C. Antipsychotics
D. Stimulants
✅ **Answer: A**

Q425. Short-term goal?
A. Reduce frequency/intensity of panic attacks + improve function
B. Cure panic in one session
C. Ignore triggers
D. Avoid exposure
✅ **Answer: A**

Q426. Risk monitoring?
A. Functional impairment, avoidance, SI
B. IQ only
C. Attendance only

D. None
✅ **Answer: A**

Q427. Family/collateral involvement?
A. Psychoeducation about panic and support strategies
B. Avoid family
C. Assign blame
D. Overprotect client
✅ **Answer: A**

Q428. Documentation priority?
A. Panic triggers, intensity, interventions, functional impact
B. Therapist opinion only
C. Ignore functional data
D. General notes only
✅ **Answer: A**

Q429. Cultural consideration?
A. Explore beliefs about anxiety, avoidance, and coping
B. Ignore culture
C. Apply generic norms
D. Force compliance
✅ **Answer: A**

Q430. Progress tracking?
A. Panic logs + GAD-7 + functional monitoring
B. MMSE only
C. LSAS
D. YMRS
✅ **Answer: A**

CASE 431–440 — Adult Bipolar II + Relationship Stress

Client: 29-year-old female. Mood swings (depression 2 weeks, hypomania 3 days), irritability, sleep disruption, relational conflict. PHQ-9 = 16, YMRS = 10.

Q431. Likely diagnosis?
A. Bipolar II

B. MDD
C. Cyclothymia
D. Borderline Personality Disorder
✅**Answer: A**

Q432. First assessment step?
A. Track mood episodes + functional impact
B. Focus only on relational conflict
C. Ignore hypomanic symptoms
D. Psychoanalysis
✅**Answer: A**

Q433. Evidence-based therapy?
A. CBT for bipolar disorder + mood monitoring
B. Hypnosis
C. EMDR
D. Psychoanalysis only
✅**Answer: A**

Q434. Medication coordination?
A. Mood stabilizer consultation with psychiatrist
B. Prescribe SSRI independently
C. Avoid medications
D. Benzodiazepines long-term
✅**Answer: A**

Q435. Short-term goal?
A. Stabilize sleep + mood + reduce irritability
B. Immediate elimination of mood swings
C. Ignore conflict
D. Avoid monitoring
✅**Answer: A**

Q436. Risk monitoring?
A. SI, impulsivity, relational conflict
B. IQ only
C. Ignore past episodes
D. Physical fitness only

✅**Answer: A**

Q437. Family involvement?
A. Psychoeducation on mood recognition + stress management
B. Exclude family
C. Punitive strategies
D. Ignore relational context
✅**Answer: A**

Q438. Documentation priority?
A. Mood charting, interventions, functional impact
B. Therapist opinion only
C. Ignore hypomanic episodes
D. General notes only
✅**Answer: A**

Q439. Cultural consideration?
A. Explore cultural norms around emotional expression + family roles
B. Ignore culture
C. Apply generic interventions
D. Force Western norms
✅**Answer: A**

Q440. Progress tracking?
A. Mood charts + PHQ-9 + YMRS + functional assessments
B. MoCA only
C. LSAS
D. IQ only
✅**Answer: A**

CASE 441–450 — Adult Substance Use + Trauma

Client: 33-year-old male. Reports alcohol use, history of childhood trauma, intimate partner conflict, insomnia, nightmares. PHQ-9 = 17, PCL-5 = 55, AUDIT = 22.

Q441. Highest-priority focus?
A. Safety + substance stabilization + trauma treatment

B. Career counseling
C. Diet planning
D. Ignore trauma
✅ **Answer: A**

Q442. Likely diagnosis?
A. PTSD + Alcohol Use Disorder
B. MDD only
C. Bipolar II only
D. GAD only
✅ **Answer: A**

Q443. Evidence-based therapy?
A. Integrated CBT or Seeking Safety for trauma + substance
B. Psychoanalysis only
C. EMDR only
D. Family therapy only
✅ **Answer: A**

Q444. Short-term goal?
A. Reduce alcohol use + stabilize mood + reduce trauma symptoms
B. Immediate abstinence without support
C. Ignore triggers
D. Avoid therapy
✅ **Answer: A**

Q445. Long-term goal?
A. Trauma processing + relapse prevention
B. Social withdrawal encouraged
C. Avoid emotional processing
D. Only meditation
✅ **Answer: A**

Q446. Risk monitoring?
A. Suicide, relapse, interpersonal safety
B. IQ only
C. Attendance only

D. Ignore risk
✅ **Answer: A**

Q447. Medication support?
A. SSRIs for PTSD/depression + adjunct for cravings if needed
B. Benzodiazepines freely
C. Antipsychotics only
D. Stimulants
✅ **Answer: A**

Q448. Family/collateral involvement?
A. Psychoeducation + support network involvement
B. Ignore family
C. Enable substance use
D. Punitive approach
✅ **Answer: A**

Q449. Cultural consideration?
A. Explore trauma meaning in client's cultural context
B. Ignore culture
C. Apply generic Western interventions
D. Assume client's values
✅ **Answer: A**

Q450. Progress tracking?
A. AUDIT + PCL-5 + functional assessment + session tracking
B. MoCA only
C. YMRS
D. TSCC only
✅ **Answer: A**

✅ Batch 10 — Questions 451–500

CASE 451–460 — Adult GAD + Chronic Illness

Client: 50-year-old female. Reports excessive worry about health, frequent doctor visits, insomnia, fatigue. Type 2 Diabetes, hypertension. GAD-7 = 18, PHQ-9 = 12.

Q451. Likely diagnosis?
A. Generalized Anxiety Disorder
B. Major Depressive Disorder
C. Panic Disorder
D. Adjustment Disorder
✅ **Answer: A**

Q452. Initial assessment focus?
A. Functional impairment, worry patterns, medical adherence
B. Ignore physical health
C. Only mood
D. IQ test
✅ **Answer: A**

Q453. Evidence-based therapy?
A. CBT for GAD + relaxation training + problem-solving
B. Psychoanalysis
C. EMDR only
D. Hypnosis only
✅ **Answer: A**

Q454. Short-term goal?
A. Reduce worry + improve sleep + enhance daily functioning
B. Eliminate all anxiety immediately
C. Avoid doctor visits
D. Ignore triggers
✅ **Answer: A**

Q455. Medication support?
A. SSRIs if indicated
B. Benzodiazepines long-term
C. Antipsychotics only
D. Stimulants
✅ **Answer: A**

Q456. Risk monitoring?
A. SI, functional impairment, medical nonadherence
B. IQ only

C. Attendance only
D. None
✅**Answer: A**

Q457. Family/collateral involvement?
A. Education about GAD + coping support
B. Avoid family
C. Punitive approach
D. Ignore social support
✅**Answer: A**

Q458. Cultural consideration?
A. Explore beliefs about health, illness, and mental health stigma
B. Ignore culture
C. Apply generic interventions
D. Force compliance
✅**Answer: A**

Q459. Documentation priority?
A. Symptoms, interventions, functional impact, consent
B. Therapist subjective notes only
C. Ignore medical context
D. General notes
✅**Answer: A**

Q460. Progress tracking?
A. GAD-7 + sleep logs + ADL/IADL monitoring
B. MoCA only
C. LSAS
D. YMRS
✅**Answer: A**

CASE 461–470 — Adolescent Anxiety + School Avoidance

Client: 14-year-old male. Severe test anxiety, avoidance of school, panic attacks before exams. PHQ-9 = 11, GAD-7 = 16.

Q461. Likely diagnosis?

A. GAD
B. Panic Disorder
C. Social Anxiety Disorder
D. OCD
✅**Answer: A**

Q462. Initial intervention?
A. CBT + coping skills + exposure to school
B. Psychoanalysis
C. Hypnosis
D. Supportive counseling only
✅**Answer: A**

Q463. School coordination?
A. Collaborate with counselor for accommodations
B. Ignore school
C. Punitive approach
D. Avoid communication
✅**Answer: A**

Q464. Short-term goal?
A. Reduce panic/anxiety + increase attendance
B. Eliminate all anxiety immediately
C. Ignore attendance
D. Focus only on academics
✅**Answer: A**

Q465. Risk monitoring?
A. Functional impairment, SI, panic severity
B. IQ only
C. Physical exam only
D. Ignore risk
✅**Answer: A**

Q466. Family involvement?
A. Psychoeducation + supportive coping strategies
B. Avoid family
C. Punitive approach

D. Ignore family context
✅**Answer: A**

Q467. Cultural sensitivity?
A. Explore cultural beliefs about education, anxiety, and support
B. Ignore culture
C. Apply generic interventions
D. Force compliance
✅**Answer: A**

Q468. Evidence-based adjunct?
A. Relaxation + breathing exercises + gradual exposure
B. Isolation
C. Confrontational techniques
D. Only medication
✅**Answer: A**

Q469. Documentation priority?
A. Symptoms, interventions, functional impact, consent
B. Therapist opinion only
C. Ignore school impact
D. General notes
✅**Answer: A**

Q470. Progress tracking?
A. GAD-7 + panic logs + attendance monitoring
B. PHQ-A only
C. MoCA
D. LSAS
✅**Answer: A**

CASE 471–480 — Adult Bipolar II + Work Stress

Client: 35-year-old male. Mood swings (2 weeks depression, 3–4 days hypomania), irritability, sleep disruption, workplace conflict. PHQ-9 = 17, YMRS = 12.

Q471. Likely diagnosis?
A. Bipolar II

B. MDD
C. Cyclothymia
D. Borderline Personality Disorder
✅ **Answer: A**

Q472. First assessment step?
A. Track mood episodes + functional impact
B. Focus only on workplace conflict
C. Ignore hypomanic symptoms
D. Psychoanalysis
✅ **Answer: A**

Q473. Evidence-based therapy?
A. CBT for bipolar disorder + mood monitoring
B. Hypnosis
C. EMDR
D. Psychoanalysis only
✅ **Answer: A**

Q474. Medication coordination?
A. Mood stabilizer consultation
B. SSRI monotherapy independently
C. Avoid medications
D. Benzodiazepines long-term
✅ **Answer: A**

Q475. Short-term goal?
A. Stabilize sleep, mood, and work performance
B. Eliminate mood swings immediately
C. Ignore irritability
D. Avoid monitoring
✅ **Answer: A**

Q476. Risk monitoring?
A. SI, impulsivity, workplace conflicts
B. IQ only
C. Ignore past episodes
D. Physical fitness only

✅**Answer: A**

Q477. Family involvement?
A. Psychoeducation on mood patterns + stress management
B. Exclude family
C. Punitive strategies
D. Ignore relational context
✅**Answer: A**

Q478. Cultural consideration?
A. Explore beliefs about emotional expression, gender roles, and work norms
B. Ignore culture
C. Force Western norms
D. Apply generic interventions
✅**Answer: A**

Q479. Documentation priority?
A. Mood charting + interventions + functional impact
B. Therapist opinion only
C. Ignore hypomanic episodes
D. General notes
✅**Answer: A**

Q480. Progress tracking?
A. Mood charts + PHQ-9 + YMRS + functional assessment
B. MoCA only
C. LSAS
D. IQ only
✅**Answer: A**

CASE 481–490 — Adult Substance Use + Depression

Client: 40-year-old female. Reports alcohol use (daily), low mood, job impairment, social withdrawal. PHQ-9 = 19, AUDIT = 25.

Q481. Likely diagnosis?
A. Major Depressive Disorder + Alcohol Use Disorder

B. GAD
C. Bipolar II
D. Panic Disorder
✅ **Answer: A**

Q482. Initial priority?
A. Safety + substance assessment + functional impairment
B. Psychoanalysis
C. Ignore substance use
D. Focus only on depression
✅ **Answer: A**

Q483. Evidence-based therapy?
A. Integrated CBT for depression + substance use
B. EMDR only
C. Supportive counseling alone
D. Hypnosis only
✅ **Answer: A**

Q484. Short-term goal?
A. Reduce drinking + improve daily functioning
B. Immediate abstinence without support
C. Ignore work impairment
D. Avoid family
✅ **Answer: A**

Q485. Risk assessment includes?
A. Suicide, relapse triggers, medical consequences
B. Only mood
C. Only substance quantity
D. None
✅ **Answer: A**

Q486. Family involvement?
A. Psychoeducation + support for recovery
B. Avoid family
C. Enable drinking
D. Punitive approach

✅**Answer: A**

Q487. Medication support?
A. SSRIs for depression + adjunct if needed
B. Benzodiazepines freely
C. Stimulants
D. Antipsychotics only
✅**Answer: A**

Q488. Cultural consideration?
A. Assess beliefs about alcohol, stigma, and support networks
B. Ignore culture
C. Apply generic interventions
D. Force compliance
✅**Answer: A**

Q489. Documentation priority?
A. Symptoms, interventions, functional impact, consent
B. Therapist opinion only
C. Ignore substance data
D. General notes
✅**Answer: A**

Q490. Progress tracking?
A. PHQ-9 + AUDIT + functional logs
B. MoCA only
C. YMRS
D. LSAS
✅**Answer: A**

CASE 491–500 — Older Adult Anxiety + Health Concerns

Client: 70-year-old male. Reports excessive worry about health, sleep disturbance, poor appetite, functional decline. PHQ-9 = 14, GAD-7 = 16.

Q491. Likely diagnosis?
A. Generalized Anxiety Disorder
B. Major Depressive Disorder

C. Adjustment Disorder
D. Panic Disorder
✅**Answer: A**

Q492. Assessment focus?
A. Cognitive function, ADLs/IADLs, functional impairment, safety
B. Ignore physical health
C. Only mood
D. IQ test
✅**Answer: A**

Q493. Evidence-based therapy?
A. CBT for anxiety + relaxation training + problem-solving
B. Psychoanalysis
C. Hypnosis only
D. EMDR only
✅**Answer: A**

Q494. Short-term goal?
A. Reduce worry + improve sleep + enhance daily functioning
B. Cure anxiety immediately
C. Ignore ADL deficits
D. Focus only on physical health
✅**Answer: A**

Q495. Medication support?
A. SSRIs if indicated, monitor for medical interactions
B. Benzodiazepines long-term
C. Stimulants
D. Antipsychotics only
✅**Answer: A**

Q496. Risk monitoring?
A. Falls, SI, functional decline, medical adherence
B. IQ only
C. Attendance only
D. None

✅**Answer: A**

Q497. Family/collateral involvement?
A. Education + support for ADLs, safety planning
B. Avoid family
C. Punitive strategies
D. Ignore caregiving context
✅**Answer: A**

Q498. Cultural consideration?
A. Explore beliefs about aging, illness, and support systems
B. Ignore culture
C. Apply generic norms
D. Force compliance
✅**Answer: A**

Q499. Documentation priority?
A. Symptoms, interventions, functional impact, consent
B. Therapist opinion only
C. Ignore medical context
D. General notes only
✅**Answer: A**

Q500. Progress tracking?
A. GAD-7 + PHQ-9 + ADL/IADL measures + functional assessment
B. MoCA only
C. LSAS
D

✅**Batch 11 — Questions 501–550**

CASE 501–510 — Adult Depression + Social Withdrawal

Client: 42-year-old female. Reports low mood, loss of interest in hobbies, social isolation, fatigue, difficulty concentrating. PHQ-9 = 21.

Q501. Likely diagnosis?

A. Major Depressive Disorder
B. GAD
C. Bipolar II
D. Adjustment Disorder
✅**Answer: A**

Q502. Initial assessment focus?
A. Functional impairment, mood severity, social withdrawal
B. Ignore daily functioning
C. Only mood
D. IQ test
✅**Answer: A**

Q503. Evidence-based therapy?
A. CBT + behavioral activation
B. Psychoanalysis only
C. Hypnosis only
D. EMDR only
✅**Answer: A**

Q504. Short-term goal?
A. Increase engagement in pleasurable activities + improve daily functioning
B. Eliminate depressive symptoms immediately
C. Avoid social interaction
D. Focus only on fatigue
✅**Answer: A**

Q505. Medication support?
A. SSRIs if indicated
B. Benzodiazepines long-term
C. Stimulants
D. Antipsychotics only
✅**Answer: A**

Q506. Risk monitoring?
A. Suicide ideation, functional impairment, social isolation
B. IQ only

C. Attendance only
D. Ignore risk
✅ **Answer: A**

Q507. Family/collateral involvement?
A. Psychoeducation about depression + support for engagement
B. Avoid family
C. Punitive strategies
D. Ignore social support
✅ **Answer: A**

Q508. Cultural sensitivity?
A. Explore cultural beliefs about mental health, stigma, and social norms
B. Ignore culture
C. Apply generic interventions
D. Force compliance
✅ **Answer: A**

Q509. Documentation priority?
A. Symptoms, interventions, functional impact, consent
B. Therapist opinion only
C. Ignore social impairment
D. General notes
✅ **Answer: A**

Q510. Progress tracking?
A. PHQ-9 + activity logs + functional assessment
B. MoCA only
C. LSAS
D. YMRS
✅ **Answer: A**

CASE 511–520 — Adolescent Anxiety + Peer Conflict

Client: 15-year-old male. Reports persistent worry about peer judgment, avoidance of social events, irritability. GAD-7 = 17, PHQ-9 = 12.

Q511. Likely diagnosis?
A. Generalized Anxiety Disorder
B. Social Anxiety Disorder
C. Panic Disorder
D. OCD
✅ **Answer: A**

Q512. Initial intervention?
A. CBT for anxiety + coping skills + exposure exercises
B. Psychoanalysis
C. Hypnosis only
D. Supportive counseling alone
✅ **Answer: A**

Q513. School coordination?
A. Collaborate with counselor for accommodations and support
B. Ignore school context
C. Punitive approach
D. Avoid communication
✅ **Answer: A**

Q514. Short-term goal?
A. Reduce worry + improve school attendance + social engagement
B. Eliminate all anxiety immediately
C. Ignore avoidance
D. Focus only on academics
✅ **Answer: A**

Q515. Risk monitoring?
A. Functional impairment, school refusal, self-harm
B. IQ only
C. Attendance only
D. Ignore risk
✅ **Answer: A**

Q516. Family involvement?
A. Psychoeducation + strategies to support coping and

communication
B. Avoid family
C. Punitive approach
D. Ignore family context
✅ **Answer: A**

Q517. Cultural sensitivity?
A. Explore beliefs about social norms, peer relationships, and mental health
B. Ignore culture
C. Apply generic interventions
D. Force compliance
✅ **Answer: A**

Q518. Evidence-based adjunct?
A. Relaxation exercises + gradual exposure + coping skills
B. Isolation
C. Confrontational techniques
D. Only medication
✅ **Answer: A**

Q519. Documentation priority?
A. Symptoms, interventions, functional impact, consent
B. Therapist opinion only
C. Ignore school impact
D. General notes
✅ **Answer: A**

Q520. Progress tracking?
A. GAD-7 + PHQ-9 + school attendance + functional logs
B. MoCA only
C. YMRS
D. LSAS
✅ **Answer: A**

CASE 521–530 — Adult Panic Disorder + Work Stress

Client: 33-year-old female. Panic attacks at work, chest tightness, dizziness, avoidance of meetings. No cardiac history.

Q521. Likely diagnosis?
A. Panic Disorder
B. GAD
C. Social Anxiety Disorder
D. OCD
✅**Answer: A**

Q522. Rule-out step?
A. Medical evaluation for cardiac issues
B. Ignore physical symptoms
C. MRI only
D. Psychoanalysis first
✅**Answer: A**

Q523. Evidence-based therapy?
A. CBT + interoceptive exposure
B. Hypnosis only
C. Psychoanalysis only
D. EMDR only
✅**Answer: A**

Q524. Medication support?
A. SSRIs
B. Benzodiazepines alone long-term
C. Stimulants
D. Antipsychotics
✅**Answer: A**

Q525. Short-term goal?
A. Reduce panic frequency/intensity + increase functional work participation
B. Eliminate panic immediately
C. Avoid triggers entirely
D. Ignore work impairment
✅**Answer: A**

Q526. Risk monitoring?

A. Functional impairment, SI, avoidance behaviors
B. IQ only
C. Attendance only
D. None
✅ **Answer: A**

Q527. Family/collateral involvement?
A. Psychoeducation on panic + supportive strategies
B. Avoid family
C. Assign blame
D. Overprotect client
✅ **Answer: A**

Q528. Cultural consideration?
A. Explore beliefs about anxiety, health, and work
B. Ignore culture
C. Force Western norms
D. Apply generic interventions
✅ **Answer: A**

Q529. Documentation priority?
A. Panic triggers, interventions, functional impact
B. Therapist opinion only
C. Ignore work impact
D. General notes
✅ **Answer: A**

Q530. Progress tracking?
A. Panic logs + GAD-7 + functional assessments
B. MoCA only
C. LSAS
D. YMRS
✅ **Answer: A**

CASE 531–540 — Adult Bipolar II + Relationship Strain

Client: 28-year-old male. Depressive episodes 2 weeks, hypomania 3–4 days, irritability, sleep disturbance, relational conflict. PHQ-9 = 16, YMRS = 10.

Q531. Likely diagnosis?
A. Bipolar II
B. MDD
C. Cyclothymia
D. Borderline Personality Disorder
✅**Answer: A**

Q532. First assessment step?
A. Track mood + functional impact
B. Focus only on relational conflict
C. Ignore hypomania
D. Psychoanalysis
✅**Answer: A**

Q533. Evidence-based therapy?
A. CBT for bipolar disorder + mood monitoring
B. Hypnosis
C. EMDR only
D. Psychoanalysis
✅**Answer: A**

Q534. Medication coordination?
A. Mood stabilizer consultation
B. SSRI monotherapy independently
C. Avoid medications
D. Benzodiazepines long-term
✅**Answer: A**

Q535. Short-term goal?
A. Stabilize sleep, mood, and relational functioning
B. Eliminate mood swings immediately
C. Ignore irritability
D. Avoid monitoring
✅**Answer: A**

Q536. Risk monitoring?
A. SI, impulsivity, relational conflict

B. IQ only
C. Ignore past episodes
D. Physical health only
✅ **Answer: A**

Q537. Family involvement?
A. Psychoeducation + support for stress management
B. Exclude family
C. Punitive strategies
D. Ignore relational context
✅ **Answer: A**

Q538. Cultural consideration?
A. Explore beliefs about emotional expression, family roles, and relationships
B. Ignore culture
C. Force Western norms
D. Apply generic interventions
✅ **Answer: A**

Q539. Documentation priority?
A. Mood charting + interventions + functional impact
B. Therapist opinion only
C. Ignore hypomania
D. General notes
✅ **Answer: A**

Q540. Progress tracking?
A. Mood charts + PHQ-9 + YMRS + functional assessments
B. MoCA only
C. LSAS
D. IQ only
✅ **Answer: A**

CASE 541–550 — Adult Substance Use + Trauma

Client: 36-year-old female. Reports alcohol use (daily), childhood trauma, nightmares, relational conflict. PHQ-9 = 18,

PCL-5 = 54, AUDIT = 24.

Q541. Highest-priority focus?
A. Safety + trauma stabilization + substance use
B. Career counseling
C. Diet planning
D. Ignore trauma
✅ **Answer: A**

Q542. Initial priority?
A. Safety + substance assessment + trauma impact
B. Psychoanalysis only
C. Ignore substance use
D. Focus only on depression
✅ **Answer: A**

Q543. Evidence-based therapy?
A. Integrated CBT for trauma + substance use (e.g., Seeking Safety)
B. EMDR only
C. Supportive counseling alone
D. Hypnosis only
✅ **Answer: A**

Q544. Short-term goal?
A. Reduce alcohol use + stabilize mood + reduce trauma symptoms
B. Immediate abstinence without support
C. Ignore relational conflicts
D. Avoid therapy
✅ **Answer: A**

Q545. Long-term goal?
A. Trauma processing + relapse prevention + functional improvement
B. Social withdrawal encouraged
C. Avoid emotional processing
D. Only meditation

✅ **Answer: A**

Q546. Risk assessment includes?
A. Suicide, relapse triggers, interpersonal safety
B. Only mood
C. Only substance quantity
D. None
✅ **Answer: A**

Q547. Medication support?
A. SSRIs for PTSD/depression + adjunct for cravings if indicated
B. Benzodiazepines freely
C. Stimulants
D. Antipsychotics only
✅ **Answer: A**

Q548. Family/collateral involvement?
A. Psychoeducation + support network engagement
B. Ignore family
C. Enable substance use
D. Punitive approach
✅ **Answer: A**

Q549. Cultural consideration?
A. Explore trauma meaning and substance use norms in client's cultural context
B. Ignore culture
C. Apply generic Western interventions
D. Assume client's values
✅ **Answer: A**

Q550. Progress tracking?
A. AUDIT + PCL-5 + session tracking + functional assessment
B. MoCA only
C. YMRS
D. TSCC only
✅ **Answer: A**

Chapter 10 : NCMHCE Flash Cards

NCMHCE Flashcards – Set 1 (Core Concepts & Scenarios)

(Training Manual Style for Practical Recall)

1⃣Diagnostic Reasoning

Q: What is the *first* step in differential diagnosis during an NCMHCE case?
A: Identify the client's **primary presenting symptoms** and **rule out medical causes** before selecting a DSM-5 diagnosis.

Pro Tip : Always consider *substance use, medical conditions, and grief* before labeling something as a mental disorder.
Hidden Pitfall : Jumping to the "obvious" diagnosis (e.g., assuming depression when it's actually bipolar II).

2⃣Suicide Risk Assessment

Q: What are the 4 key areas of suicide risk assessment?
A: Plan, Means, Intent, and History.

Pro Tip : Always ask directly and document word-for-word client responses.
Hidden Pitfall : Assuming that "no plan" means "no risk." Passive suicidal ideation still requires safety planning.

3⃣Treatment Planning

Q: What 3 elements must every treatment goal have?
A: Specific, Measurable, and Achievable objectives tied to diagnosis.

Pro Tip : Link each goal to a specific *intervention* — the NCMHCE often scores you on congruence between problem, goal, and intervention.

Hidden Pitfall : Writing vague goals like "Client will feel better.” Instead, say “Client will identify and challenge 3 cognitive distortions per week.”

4□Counseling Theories Overview

Q: Which theory focuses most on *unconditional positive regard*?
A: Humanistic (Person-Centered Therapy) by Carl Rogers.

Pro Tip : On exam cases, look for keywords like “self-acceptance,” “growth,” or “empathy” to cue this orientation.

Hidden Pitfall : Confusing “being nice” with true empathy. Person-centered therapy requires deep, active listening — not passive kindness.

5□Cognitive Behavioral Therapy (CBT)

Q: What is the basic CBT triangle?
A: Thoughts → Feelings → Behaviors.

Pro Tip : When you see distorted self-talk in a case vignette (e.g., “I always fail”), think CBT.

Hidden Pitfall : Using CBT too early with trauma clients — insight without safety can trigger flooding.

6□Crisis Intervention

Q: What’s the first priority in any crisis case?
A: Ensure client safety. Assess for immediate danger to self or others.

Pro Tip : Use short-term, directive interventions focused on stabilization.
Hidden Pitfall : Jumping into long-term therapy planning before the crisis is resolved.

7□ Ethical Decision-Making

Q: What are the 6 basic steps in ethical decision-making?
A: Identify → Review Codes → Consult → Explore Options → Decide → Document.

Pro Tip : Always consult and document — even if you're confident in your choice.
Hidden Pitfall : Acting too quickly out of fear — ethics require reflection, not reaction.

8□Informed Consent

Q: What must be included in informed consent?
A: Purpose, process, risks, benefits, confidentiality limits, and client rights.

Pro Tip : Revisit consent throughout treatment, not just at intake.
Hidden Pitfall : Forgetting to explain *limits of confidentiality* during emergencies (duty to warn/protect).

9□Multicultural Counseling

Q: What's the most important counselor skill in multicultural work?
A: Cultural humility — curiosity over expertise.

Pro Tip ?: Use the "ASK model": Ask, Seek, Know.
Hidden Pitfall : Overgeneralizing cultural values ("All clients from X culture value family first").

Group Counseling

Q: What's the "here and now" principle in group therapy?
A: Focus on what's happening *within the group interaction* in real time.

Pro Tip : Process comments like "I notice you withdraw when others get emotional" are scored highly.

Hidden Pitfall : Letting one member dominate — exam scoring penalizes lack of group management.

11□ Substance Use Cases

Q: What is the first step in treating substance use?
A: Assess readiness to change (using stages of change model).

Pro Tip : Match your intervention to their stage — e.g., use *Motivational Interviewing* if they're ambivalent.
Hidden Pitfall : Pushing abstinence in precontemplation phase — it backfires.

12□Documentation

Q: What is the SOAP note structure?
A: Subjective, Objective, Assessment, Plan.

Pro Tip : Write as if another clinician must continue care tomorrow — clarity is professionalism.
Hidden Pitfall : Including client judgments (e.g., "Client was manipulative"). Stick to observable behavior.

13□Boundaries and Dual Relationships

Q: What's the ethical rule on dual relationships?
A: Avoid when possible; manage transparently and document when unavoidable.

Pro Tip : The *potential for harm* determines whether a dual relationship is unethical.
Hidden Pitfall : Assuming all dual relationships are forbidden — some (e.g., small-town overlap) can be managed ethically.

14□ Family Systems

Q: What is triangulation in family therapy?
A: When two family members pull in a third to reduce tension between them.

Pro Tip : Help families communicate directly instead of through alliances.
Hidden Pitfall : Taking sides — neutrality is the therapist's power position.

15□Career Counseling

Q: What is Holland's theory of vocational choice based on?
A: Personality–environment fit (RIASEC model: Realistic, Investigative, Artistic, Social, Enterprising, Conventional).

Pro Tip : When a client feels "bored" or "misaligned" at work, look for poor Holland fit.
Hidden Pitfall : Assuming higher pay equals better fit — satisfaction drives success, not salary.

16□Case Conceptualization

Q: What three pillars define a strong case conceptualization?
A: Problem identification, theoretical explanation, and treatment plan linkage.

Pro Tip : Tie interventions back to theory on the NCMHCE — it shows clinical reasoning.
Hidden Pitfall : Giving generic advice that isn't tied to the diagnosis or theoretical model.

17□Progress Evaluation

Q: How often should you re-evaluate treatment progress?
A: Every 4–6 sessions or whenever symptoms change.

Pro Tip : Use measurable outcomes (e.g., "decrease panic attacks from 5/week to 1/week").
Hidden Pitfall : Continuing ineffective interventions due to counselor comfort zone.

18□Termination

Q: What are the key steps in proper termination?
A: Review goals, celebrate progress, plan maintenance, provide referrals.

Pro Tip : Frame termination as growth, not abandonment.
Hidden Pitfall : Ending abruptly or emotionally detaching to avoid your own discomfort.

19□Confidentiality Exceptions

Q: Name three major limits to confidentiality.
A: Harm to self/others, abuse of vulnerable persons, court order.

Pro Tip : State these clearly in the first session — transparency builds trust.
Hidden Pitfall : Overpromising "complete confidentiality" — always outline exceptions upfront.

20□ Self-Care for Counselors

Q: Why is self-care an ethical issue?
A: Counselor impairment directly affects client welfare and ethical competence.

Pro Tip ?: Create a self-care plan — physical, emotional, and professional domains.
Hidden Pitfall : Believing burnout "won't happen to me." Compassion fatigue creeps in gradually.

✅**Study Strategy**

- Practice **10–15 flashcards daily**.
- After reading each, **apply it to a brief client scenario** (that's exactly how NCMHCE frames questions).
- Mix in **theory-based** and **crisis-based** questions in each study session.

Let's continue with NCMHCE Flashcards – Set 2: Advanced Scenario-Based Practice.
These simulate the *decision-making style* of the real exam — where you apply clinical reasoning, ethics, and interventions to case vignettes.
Each flashcard includes a Scenario, Question, Best Action, Pro Tip, and Hidden Pitfall.

NCMHCE Flashcards – Set 2: Advanced Scenarios

1□Anxiety vs. OCD

Scenario:
A 29-year-old client reports excessive worry about cleanliness. She spends 2–3 hours daily washing her hands but knows it's irrational.

Question: What's the most likely diagnosis?
Best Action: Diagnose **Obsessive-Compulsive Disorder (OCD)** — not Generalized Anxiety Disorder.
Pro Tip : The presence of *rituals* (compulsions) that relieve anxiety distinguishes OCD.
Hidden Pitfall : Labeling all anxiety-based behaviors as GAD without identifying compulsive patterns.

2□Major Depression or Grief?

Scenario:
A 45-year-old client reports sadness, loss of appetite, and insomnia 3 weeks after his spouse's death.

Question: What's your clinical impression?
Best Action: Diagnose **Uncomplicated Bereavement**, not Major Depressive Disorder (yet).
Pro Tip ?: Grief allows for fluctuating emotions — depression is persistent, pervasive hopelessness.
Hidden Pitfall : Pathologizing normal grief within the first few

weeks of loss.

3□Crisis & Safety Planning

Scenario:
A college student confides suicidal thoughts but no specific plan or means.

Question: What's your immediate next step?
Best Action: Develop a collaborative safety plan and increase contact frequency.
Pro Tip : The NCMHCE rewards steps that *enhance safety + empowerment*, not hospitalization if risk is low.
Hidden Pitfall : Overreacting by involuntarily hospitalizing without clear imminent danger.

4□Couples Case

Scenario:
A couple argues constantly; one partner says, "He never listens, and I'm done trying."

Question: What intervention should you use first?
Best Action: Establish communication rules and model reflective listening.
Pro Tip ?: Early structure builds safety before exploring deep content.
Hidden Pitfall : Diving into family-of-origin issues before stabilizing the relationship dynamic.

5□Adolescent Substance Use

Scenario:
A 16-year-old admits using marijuana "to calm down," denies problem behavior.

Question: What's your most effective approach?
Best Action: Use **Motivational Interviewing (MI)** to explore ambivalence.

Pro Tip ?: Match the client's *stage of change* — here, "precontemplation."
Hidden Pitfall : Lecturing or confronting — it triggers resistance and disengagement.

6□Trauma Case

Scenario:
A veteran reports nightmares, flashbacks, and hypervigilance since returning from deployment.

Question: Which intervention is best *initially*?
Best Action: Focus on **stabilization and grounding techniques** before trauma processing.
Pro Tip ?: Safety before story — establish control over triggers first.
Hidden Pitfall : Jumping into exposure therapy before the client has coping tools.

7□ Career Counseling

Scenario:
A client feels "unfulfilled" in a high-paying finance job. Career testing shows high Artistic and Social scores.

Question: What theory guides this case?
Best Action: Apply **Holland's RIASEC model** — identify a better personality-environment fit.
Pro Tip : Look for *incongruence between values and work environment.*
Hidden Pitfall : Assuming dissatisfaction = burnout rather than poor vocational match.

8□ Older Adult

Scenario:
A 72-year-old widow reports memory lapses and sadness. She forgets appointments and repeats questions.

Question: What's your next clinical step?
Best Action: Refer for medical evaluation to rule out neurocognitive disorder.
Pro Tip ?: Always rule out physiological causes before diagnosing depression or anxiety.
Hidden Pitfall : Assuming cognitive decline is purely "emotional" or grief-related.

9□Group Therapy

Scenario:
In a therapy group, one member dominates every session. Others withdraw.

Question: What's the best counselor response?
Best Action: Address the process — gently explore how the member's behavior affects the group.
Pro Tip ?: Use "here-and-now" feedback to promote self-awareness.
Hidden Pitfall : Ignoring it to "keep peace" — avoidance erodes group cohesion.

Ethical Dilemma

Scenario:
A client reveals ongoing domestic violence but asks you not to report it.

Question: What should you do?
Best Action: Follow mandated reporting laws and inform the client transparently.
Pro Tip ?: Always prioritize safety and legal duty — then offer emotional support.
Hidden Pitfall : Keeping confidentiality to "protect trust." It's both unethical and illegal in this case.

11□ Multicultural Scenario

Scenario:
A client from a collectivist culture hesitates to make independent decisions in therapy.

Question: How should you adapt your approach?
Best Action: Incorporate **family and community context** into goal setting.
Pro Tip ?: Flex your counseling model to fit cultural worldview — not the other way around.
Hidden Pitfall : Labeling dependency as pathology; it may reflect cultural harmony values.

12□Co-Occurring Disorders

Scenario:
A client presents with depression and heavy alcohol use.

Question: What's your treatment focus?
Best Action: Use an **integrated dual-diagnosis approach** — treat both concurrently.
Pro Tip ?: Address motivation for sobriety while managing depressive symptoms.
Hidden Pitfall : Treating one disorder while ignoring the other — relapse risk skyrockets.

13□Psychodynamic Example

Scenario:
A client repeatedly arrives late and blames traffic, though sessions are afternoon.

Question: How might you interpret this behavior?
Best Action: Explore resistance or transference rather than confronting immediately.
Pro Tip ?: In psychodynamic therapy, behavior often symbolizes deeper emotion.
Hidden Pitfall : Viewing lateness as "noncompliance" instead

of unconscious communication.

14□CBT Example

Scenario:
A client says, "I'm a failure; I'll never get better."

Question: Which CBT intervention applies?
Best Action: Identify and challenge cognitive distortions ("all-or-nothing thinking").
Pro Tip ?: Help client gather *evidence for and against* their belief.
Hidden Pitfall : Reassuring without restructuring thoughts — it reinforces helplessness.

15□Documentation Scenario

Scenario:
You must write a progress note after a crisis session.

Question: What should your note include?
Best Action: Document **risk assessment, interventions, and client response.**
Pro Tip ?: Notes may be reviewed legally — stay factual, objective, concise.
Hidden Pitfall : Including your opinions or speculations ("Client overreacted").

✅Study Tip

When using these flashcards:

- Read the **scenario first** — decide what you'd do.
- Then check your answer against the **Best Action** and **Pitfall**.
- For mastery, explain *why* your action is justified under the **ACA Code of Ethics** or your chosen theoretical model.

here's NCMHCE Flashcards – Set 3: Diagnostic Reasoning & Treatment Planning.

This set focuses on **DSM-5 differential diagnosis clues** and how to select the most appropriate **intervention or next step** — exactly what's tested in the **Information Gathering (IG)** and **Decision-Making (DM)** portions of the exam.

Each flashcard includes:

- ***Scenario*** *(brief vignette)*
- ***Question*** *(your reasoning task)*
- ***Best Action or Diagnosis***
- ***Pro Tip ?***
- ***Hidden Pitfall***

NCMHCE Flashcards – Set 3: Diagnostic Reasoning & Treatment Planning

1□ Major Depressive Disorder (MDD) vs. Persistent Depressive Disorder (PDD)

Scenario:
A 36-year-old client reports low mood "for years," low energy, and poor self-esteem but no major impairment spikes.

Question: Which diagnosis fits best?
Best Action: Persistent Depressive Disorder (Dysthymia).
Pro Tip ?: MDD = episodic (≥2 weeks of severe symptoms). PDD = chronic (≥2 years, mild to moderate).
Hidden Pitfall : Calling long-term sadness "MDD" without noting duration and intensity.

2□Bipolar II vs. Cyclothymic Disorder

Scenario:
Client has alternating "highs" and "lows" for 3 years, but highs

never cause major impairment.

Question: Which diagnosis is most accurate?
Best Action: Cyclothymic Disorder.
Pro Tip : Bipolar II has *major depressive episodes* and *hypomania*. Cyclothymia = subthreshold mood swings.
Hidden Pitfall : Over-diagnosing Bipolar II when no full depressive episode is present.

3□Generalized Anxiety Disorder (GAD) vs. Panic Disorder

Scenario:
Client reports chronic tension, restlessness, and "worrying about everything," not specific panic attacks.

Question: Diagnosis?
Best Action: Generalized Anxiety Disorder.
Pro Tip ?: GAD = pervasive worry; Panic = discrete, sudden attacks.
Hidden Pitfall : Confusing constant anxiety (GAD) with episodic surges (Panic Disorder).

4□Social Anxiety vs. Avoidant Personality Disorder

Scenario:
Client avoids parties, fears embarrassment, but functions well at work with small groups.

Question: Likely diagnosis?
Best Action: Social Anxiety Disorder.
Pro Tip : Personality disorders show *pervasive inflexibility* across all settings.
Hidden Pitfall : Mistaking situational anxiety for a stable personality trait.

5□PTSD vs. Acute Stress Disorder

Scenario:
Client witnessed a car accident two weeks ago; reports

flashbacks and nightmares.

Question: Correct diagnosis?
Best Action: Acute Stress Disorder (if symptoms < 1 month).
Pro Tip ?: Duration defines difference — PTSD = symptoms persist ≥1 month.
Hidden Pitfall : Mislabeling as PTSD too early.

6□Borderline Personality Disorder (BPD)

Scenario:
Client describes unstable relationships, fear of abandonment, impulsive spending, and self-harm gestures.

Question: What's the best conceptual fit?
Best Action: Borderline Personality Disorder.
Pro Tip ?: Emotional instability + frantic efforts to avoid abandonment = BPD hallmarks.
Hidden Pitfall : Dismissing symptoms as "just trauma" without noting chronic relational patterns.

7□ADHD in Adults

Scenario:
A 32-year-old reports disorganization, procrastination, and "never finishing tasks." Onset since childhood.

Question: Most appropriate next step?
Best Action: Rule out other causes (depression, anxiety) → then consider ADHD evaluation.
Pro Tip ?: Confirm *childhood onset* — ADHD doesn't start in adulthood.
Hidden Pitfall : Diagnosing ADHD when symptoms stem from stress or sleep deprivation.

8□ Adjustment Disorder vs. Major Depression

Scenario:
Client reports sadness, sleep issues, and irritability after losing a

job 3 weeks ago; symptoms mild.

Question: Diagnosis?
Best Action: Adjustment Disorder with Depressed Mood.
Pro Tip ?: Triggered by identifiable stressor within 3 months, and resolves when stressor ends.
Hidden Pitfall : Diagnosing MDD when symptoms are mild and situational.

9□Substance-Induced Mood Disorder

Scenario:
Client reports depressive symptoms that began after starting heavy alcohol use.

Question: Diagnostic priority?
Best Action: Rule out substance-induced disorder before primary depression.
Pro Tip : Always consider temporal relationship: Did symptoms start *after* substance use began?
Hidden Pitfall : Treating mood disorder without addressing the substance trigger.

Obsessive-Compulsive Personality vs. OCD

Scenario:
Client is overly perfectionistic, rigid with rules, but no intrusive thoughts or compulsions.

Question: Diagnosis?
Best Action: Obsessive-Compulsive Personality Disorder (OCPD).
Pro Tip ?: OCD = anxiety-driven obsessions; OCPD = control-driven personality style.
Hidden Pitfall : Confusing orderliness with true obsessions or rituals.

11□Eating Disorders

Scenario:
Client has intense fear of gaining weight, BMI below normal, and body image distortion.

Question: Diagnosis?
Best Action: Anorexia Nervosa.
Pro Tip ?: If normal BMI with purging, think **Bulimia Nervosa** instead.
Hidden Pitfall : Assuming “normal weight” rules out eating disorder — focus on behaviors and perception.

12□ Schizophrenia Spectrum

Scenario:
Client reports auditory hallucinations, disorganized speech, and flat affect for 2 months.

Question: Diagnosis?
Best Action: Schizophreniform Disorder (duration 1–6 months).
Pro Tip ?: Schizophrenia requires ≥6 months of symptoms.
Hidden Pitfall : Jumping to schizophrenia diagnosis before the 6-month threshold.

13□Personality Disorders – General Rule

Scenario:
Client presents with lifelong relationship difficulties, lack of insight, and inflexible coping patterns.

Question: How to confirm personality disorder?
Best Action: Verify **chronicity and pervasiveness** across time and contexts.
Pro Tip ?: Personality disorders are *ego-syntonic* — clients often don’t see behavior as problematic.
Hidden Pitfall : Mistaking situational behavior for personality pathology.

14□Treatment Planning Basics

Scenario:
Client diagnosed with MDD, moderate severity.

Question: What's a good treatment plan goal?
Best Action: "Client will identify and challenge 3 cognitive distortions per week using CBT techniques."
Pro Tip ?: Goals must link to both **symptom** and **technique**.
Hidden Pitfall : Writing vague goals ("feel happier") without measurable actions.

15□ Stages of Change Model

Scenario:
Client says, "I don't think my drinking is a big deal."

Question: What stage of change is this?
Best Action: Precontemplation.
Pro Tip ?: Match intervention to stage — use **Motivational Interviewing** here.
Hidden Pitfall : Pushing for behavioral change before client readiness.

16□Crisis Plan Creation

Scenario:
Client expresses passive suicidal thoughts ("I wish I didn't wake up") but no plan or intent.

Question: Best immediate action?
Best Action: Create a **safety plan**, increase session frequency, and provide hotline numbers.
Pro Tip : Always document protective factors and coping strategies.
Hidden Pitfall : Minimizing risk because there's "no plan" — ideation still matters.

17□ Trauma-Focused Treatment Plan

Scenario:
Client with PTSD struggles with nightmares and emotional numbing.

Question: What's your early-stage focus?
Best Action: Build **stabilization and emotion-regulation skills** before trauma processing.
Pro Tip ?: Safety first, narrative later.
Hidden Pitfall : Starting exposure therapy too soon — retraumatization risk.

18□Co-Occurring Disorders Treatment Planning

Scenario:
Client diagnosed with GAD and Alcohol Use Disorder.

Question: Best plan?
Best Action: Integrated treatment: anxiety management + substance counseling simultaneously.
Pro Tip ?: Treat both — sequential care leads to relapse.
Hidden Pitfall : Referring substance treatment out and ignoring anxiety triggers.

19□Child Case Example

Scenario:
10-year-old with nightmares, clinging, and school avoidance after parental divorce.

Question: Likely diagnosis and first step?
Best Action: Adjustment Disorder with Anxiety; start **play therapy and family involvement.**
Pro Tip : Children express distress through behavior, not verbalization.
Hidden Pitfall : Labeling as "Oppositional" before considering context.

20□Documentation & Evaluation

Scenario:
You're evaluating progress for a client with panic disorder after 6 sessions.

Question: What's best practice?
Best Action: Measure **frequency, duration, and intensity** of panic attacks; update plan accordingly.
Pro Tip ?: Use standardized scales (e.g., Beck Anxiety Inventory).
Hidden Pitfall : Relying on subjective "client feels better" without quantifiable data.

✅ **Study Tip for Set 3**

- Practice identifying **DSM-5 keywords** in scenarios ("duration," "severity," "trigger," "onset").
- For each vignette, ask:
    1. What's the **most likely diagnosis**?
    2. What's the **next clinical step**?
    3. What's the **best evidence-based intervention**?
- These three layers mirror the **Information Gathering → Decision Making → Evaluation** format of NCMHCE.

Here's NCMHCE Flashcards – Set 4: Ethics, Law, and Professional Practice — designed in practical, training-manual style to help you master ethical and legal reasoning under pressure.

These cards reflect how the **NCMHCE** tests professional judgment — balancing *client welfare, ethical codes, and legal mandates*.

Each flashcard includes:

- **Scenario**

- **Question**
- **Best Action**
- **Pro Tip ?**
- **Hidden Pitfall**

NCMHCE Flashcards – Set 4: Ethics, Law & Professional Practice

1□Informed Consent

Scenario:
A new client begins counseling and asks, "Do I have to sign anything before we start?"

Question: What's required before counseling begins?
Best Action: Obtain **informed consent** outlining goals, risks, benefits, confidentiality limits, and rights.
Pro Tip : Consent is a *process*, not a one-time form — revisit it when treatment changes.
Hidden Pitfall : Skipping verbal discussion and relying only on paperwork.

2□Confidentiality & Exceptions

Scenario:
A client reveals intent to harm a coworker but refuses to let you warn anyone.

Question: What must you do?
Best Action: Breach confidentiality under the *duty to warn/protect*.
Pro Tip : Document *what was said, your reasoning, and who you notified*.
Hidden Pitfall : Waiting for explicit "plan and means" before acting — potential harm triggers duty.

3□Mandated Reporting – Child Abuse

Scenario:
A 9-year-old mentions, "My stepdad gets really mad and hits me with a belt."

Question: Next step?
Best Action: Report immediately to child protective services — mandatory by law.
Pro Tip : You don't need proof, only **reasonable suspicion**.
Hidden Pitfall : "Checking with parents first" — could endanger the child.

4□Dual Relationships

Scenario:
A client invites you to their art show after 3 months of therapy.

Question: Should you attend?
Best Action: Decline politely — avoid potential boundary confusion.
Pro Tip : If you can't avoid overlap (e.g., small town), set clear boundaries and document discussion.
Hidden Pitfall : Believing "it's harmless" — even small dual roles can compromise neutrality.

5□Competence & Scope of Practice

Scenario:
You're asked to counsel a couple struggling with infertility, but you have no training in reproductive issues.

Question: What's the ethical course of action?
Best Action: Seek supervision, consultation, or referral before proceeding.
Pro Tip : Competence is based on *training* + *experience*, not confidence.
Hidden Pitfall : Accepting the case out of guilt or pressure.

6□Record Keeping

Scenario:
A client requests a copy of their counseling notes.

Question: What's your responsibility?
Best Action: Provide **access to records** unless it would cause serious harm; offer summary if appropriate.
Pro Tip ?: Keep clinical and process notes separate.
Hidden Pitfall : Denying access without valid reason — violates ACA Code of Ethics (Section B.6).

7□Counselor Impairment

Scenario:
You've been experiencing burnout and missing documentation deadlines.

Question: What's the ethical obligation?
Best Action: Seek supervision or temporary leave to protect client welfare.
Pro Tip ?: Counselor self-care is an *ethical duty*, not a luxury.
Hidden Pitfall : "Pushing through" impairment — leads to boundary and judgment errors.

8□Supervision & Consultation

Scenario:
A supervisee discloses they're unsure how to handle a suicidal client.

Question: Supervisor's responsibility?
Best Action: Provide **immediate guidance**, ensure safety protocols, and review documentation.
Pro Tip : Supervisors share *legal and ethical responsibility* for supervisees' actions.
Hidden Pitfall : Saying "use your best judgment" without ensuring safety follow-up.

9□Telehealth Ethics

Scenario:
You're providing online counseling across state lines to a former in-state client.

Question: Is this ethical?
Best Action: Only if **licensed in the client's current state** or allowed by interstate compacts.
Pro Tip : Verify telehealth laws in *both* jurisdictions.
Hidden Pitfall : Assuming virtual delivery bypasses state licensing rules.

Termination of Services

Scenario:
A client stops attending sessions but still owes a balance.

Question: What's your ethical duty?
Best Action: Attempt **follow-up contact**, provide referrals, and document termination rationale.
Pro Tip ?: Termination = planned closure, not abandonment.
Hidden Pitfall : Ending contact abruptly without referrals or closure session.

11□Client Competence

Scenario:
A client with schizophrenia becomes disoriented and unable to give informed consent.

Question: Next step?
Best Action: Pause treatment and consult family, guardians, or medical professionals.
Pro Tip ?: Reassess capacity regularly — competence can fluctuate.
Hidden Pitfall : Continuing therapy when client cannot understand treatment decisions.

12□ Confidentiality in Group Counseling

Scenario:
During a group session, a member shares private information about another participant.

Question: Counselor response?
Best Action: Reinforce group confidentiality guidelines and process the breach.
Pro Tip : Confidentiality in groups = ethical *expectation*, not legal protection.
Hidden Pitfall : Ignoring the incident — trust in group dissolves quickly.

13□HIPAA & Electronic Records

Scenario:
You use a personal laptop to store session notes without encryption.

Question: Ethical/legal issue?
Best Action: Encrypt all client data and use secure, HIPAA-compliant software.
Pro Tip ?: Always lock devices and use two-factor authentication.
Hidden Pitfall : Assuming password protection alone is sufficient under HIPAA.

14□Cultural Competence

Scenario:
You find yourself struggling to understand a client's spiritual beliefs during grief counseling.

Question: Ethical action?
Best Action: Acknowledge limits, seek consultation, or refer if necessary.
Pro Tip : Cultural humility > cultural expertise — stay curious, not judgmental.

Hidden Pitfall : Imposing your worldview through interpretation.

15□ Confidentiality After Death

Scenario:
A deceased client's family requests therapy records.

Question: What's the correct course?
Best Action: Protect confidentiality unless legally required to release (e.g., court order).
Pro Tip ?: Client confidentiality continues after death.
Hidden Pitfall : Assuming death automatically releases privacy rights.

16□ Legal Subpoenas

Scenario:
You receive a subpoena for client records.

Question: What should you do first?
Best Action: Consult legal counsel before releasing any records.
Pro Tip : A subpoena ≠ court order; verify what's required.
Hidden Pitfall : Sending full notes without client consent or legal confirmation.

17□ Bartering in Therapy

Scenario:
A client offers handmade art in exchange for counseling sessions.

Question: Is this ethical?
Best Action: Possibly — if it's **not exploitative, culturally appropriate, and documented**.
Pro Tip ?: Evaluate potential for harm or power imbalance.
Hidden Pitfall : Accepting barter without written agreement.

18□ Working with Minors

Scenario:
A 15-year-old requests confidentiality about dating issues, but parents ask for session notes.

Question: What do you do?
Best Action: Balance confidentiality with parental rights — share general progress, not specifics.
Pro Tip : Set boundaries at intake; explain confidentiality limits to both child and parents.
Hidden Pitfall : Disclosing private details and breaching trust unnecessarily.

19□Client Abandonment

Scenario:
You plan a two-month vacation and won't be available for current clients.

Question: Ethical responsibility?
Best Action: Provide advance notice, referrals, and emergency contact coverage.
Pro Tip ?: Clients must never be left without clinical support options.
Hidden Pitfall : Leaving town without continuity planning — classic abandonment risk.

20□ Ethical Decision-Making Steps

Scenario:
You face a dilemma with no clear solution under the code.

Question: What's your process?
Best Action:

1. Identify problem
2. Review code & laws
3. Consult

4. Brainstorm options
5. Choose and act
6. Document rationale

Pro Tip : Consultation = best friend in gray-area ethics.
Hidden Pitfall : Acting quickly based on emotion instead of structured reasoning.

✅**Study Tip for Set 4**

To master Ethics on the NCMHCE:

- Memorize **when to break confidentiality** (duty to warn, protect, report).
- Know **client rights** (access to records, informed consent).
- Remember: **"When in doubt — consult, document, protect."**
- Expect **legal + ethical overlap questions** that test *judgment*, not memorization.

Here's NCMHCE Flashcards – Set 5: Crisis, Suicide, and Emergency Interventions — focused on high-stakes situations where the counselor's judgment, ethical reasoning, and clinical skills are tested under pressure.

Each card includes:

- **Scenario**
- **Question**
- **Best Action**
- **Pro Tip ?**
- **Hidden Pitfall**

NCMHCE Flashcards – Set 5: Crisis, Suicide, and Emergency Interventions

1□Suicidal Ideation – Initial Assessment

Scenario:
A 32-year-old client says, "I sometimes wish I could just disappear."

Question: What should you do first?
Best Action: Conduct a **suicide risk assessment** — ask directly about *plan, means, intent, and history.*
Pro Tip ?: Asking about suicide **does not increase risk** — it opens communication.
Hidden Pitfall : Avoiding the question out of fear or discomfort.

2□ Suicidal Client with a Plan

Scenario:
Client states, "I plan to take all my pills tonight when my roommate leaves."

Question: Next step?
Best Action: Ensure immediate safety — contact emergency services or arrange hospitalization.
Pro Tip ?: If imminent risk → *no confidentiality barrier applies.*
Hidden Pitfall : Scheduling next-day session instead of intervening immediately.

3□ Assessing Suicide Risk Factors

Scenario:
A middle-aged man lost his job, lives alone, and gave away his dog.

Question: What does this indicate?
Best Action: High risk — multiple risk factors and preparatory behaviors.

Pro Tip ?: Look for **protective factors** (social support, religion, hope) to guide intervention.
Hidden Pitfall : Overlooking "nonverbal cues" like giving away possessions.

4□ Non-Suicidal Self-Injury (NSSI)

Scenario:
A teen admits to cutting but denies wanting to die.

Question: How to proceed?
Best Action: Assess **function and triggers** of behavior; ensure safety and create coping plan.
Pro Tip ?: NSSI ≠ suicidal intent, but increases **future suicide risk**.
Hidden Pitfall : Dismissing it as "attention-seeking" — it's often emotion regulation.

5□ Homicidal Ideation

Scenario:
Client says, "If my ex ever cheats again, I'll kill her."

Question: What's your ethical duty?
Best Action: Assess threat credibility, and if specific and imminent → **duty to warn/protect**.
Pro Tip ?: Document threat details and consultation steps.
Hidden Pitfall : Ignoring vague threats that later escalate.

6□Crisis Intervention Model

Scenario:
Client in panic after losing home in a fire.

Question: What's your immediate focus?
Best Action: Use **6-Step Crisis Model** —

1. Establish safety
2. Define problem

3. Provide support
4. Explore alternatives
5. Make plan
6. Commit to action
   Pro Tip : Stabilization first; therapy later.
   Hidden Pitfall : Jumping to insight-based therapy in acute phase.

7□ Domestic Violence

Scenario:
Client shows bruises but denies abuse: “I fell down the stairs.”

Question: Counselor’s responsibility?
Best Action: Assess for safety privately; provide resources and hotlines.
Pro Tip : Avoid confronting abuser or insisting on police report — empower, don’t endanger.
Hidden Pitfall : Conducting joint sessions when abuse is suspected.

8□Child Abuse Disclosure

Scenario:
A child says, “My uncle touches me sometimes.”

Question: What’s required?
Best Action: Mandatory report to child protective services immediately.
Pro Tip : Stay calm, thank the child, don’t interrogate — you’re not the investigator.
Hidden Pitfall : Promising secrecy — never guarantee confidentiality in abuse cases.

9□ Duty to Warn/Protect

Scenario:

Client admits planning to harm a former coworker but hasn't acted yet.

Question: What's your legal obligation?
Best Action: Warn identifiable target and notify authorities if threat is credible.
Pro Tip : When in doubt — consult and document.
Hidden Pitfall : Assuming the duty applies only after a crime occurs.

Grief Crisis vs. Depression

Scenario:
A client says, "I can't stop crying since my wife died six weeks ago."

Question: What's your clinical judgment?
Best Action: Normal grief reaction — monitor for major depression (duration >2 months, suicidal thoughts, impairment).
Pro Tip ?: Validate pain, don't pathologize grief too early.
Hidden Pitfall : Mislabeling grief as a depressive disorder prematurely.

11□Panic Attack in Session

Scenario:
Client suddenly hyperventilates and says, "I can't breathe."

Question: How to respond?
Best Action: Ground and breathe — model slow breathing, reorient to present.
Pro Tip : Keep tone calm and steady; panic feeds on fear.
Hidden Pitfall : Calling emergency services immediately without assessing severity.

12□Trauma & PTSD

Scenario:
Client reports nightmares and flashbacks 3 weeks after an

assault.

Question: Diagnosis or phase?
Best Action: Acute Stress Reaction — too soon for PTSD.
Pro Tip : Early grounding and psychoeducation are key.
Hidden Pitfall : Forcing trauma narrative too early — re-traumatization risk.

13□Suicide Safety Planning

Scenario:
A client at moderate risk agrees to work on safety.

Question: What elements must safety plan include?
Best Action:

- Warning signs
- Coping strategies
- Contacts for support
- Emergency numbers
- Crisis lines
  Pro Tip ?: Have client **write or save plan on phone**.
  Hidden Pitfall : Assuming verbal agreement = safety plan.

14□ Hospitalization Decision

Scenario:
A client refuses hospitalization but expresses suicidal intent.

Question: What's your next move?
Best Action: Initiate involuntary commitment per state law if danger is imminent.
Pro Tip : Safety > autonomy when life is at risk.
Hidden Pitfall : Allowing client to leave after suicidal disclosure.

15□ Crisis Debriefing

Scenario:
You're facilitating debriefing after workplace violence incident.

Question: Primary goal?
Best Action: Normalize reactions, promote coping, and identify those needing further care.
Pro Tip : Focus on **stabilization**, not processing trauma details.
Hidden Pitfall : Encouraging in-depth storytelling too early.

16□Substance-Related Crisis

Scenario:
A client arrives intoxicated and agitated, threatening self-harm.

Question: What should you do?
Best Action: De-escalate and ensure safety — do not conduct full session.
Pro Tip ?: Safety first, treatment later — intoxication impairs consent.
Hidden Pitfall : Trying to "talk through" risk while client is impaired.

17□ Elder Abuse

Scenario:
An elderly client says, "My caregiver sometimes forgets to feed me."

Question: Next step?
Best Action: Report to Adult Protective Services (APS) — mandatory for suspected neglect.
Pro Tip : Financial and neglect abuse are often hidden; ask direct questions.
Hidden Pitfall : Believing "it's just family issues" — always investigate.

18□ School Crisis – Threats

Scenario:
Student tells you, "My friend wants to hurt people at school tomorrow."

Question: What's your obligation?
Best Action: Warn school officials and authorities immediately.
Pro Tip : Student confidentiality yields to **public safety**.
Hidden Pitfall : Waiting to "confirm" threat before reporting.

19□ Vicarious Trauma (Counselor)

Scenario:
You've been working with trauma clients and feel emotionally numb.

Question: What's happening?
Best Action: Vicarious trauma — seek supervision and self-care strategies.
Pro Tip : Regular debriefing prevents burnout.
Hidden Pitfall : Ignoring warning signs of compassion fatigue.

20□Post-Crisis Follow-Up

Scenario:
Client was hospitalized for suicidality last month and returns to counseling.

Question: What's priority in follow-up?
Best Action: Review safety plan, rebuild trust, and coordinate care with treatment team.
Pro Tip : Document re-engagement steps and ongoing risk monitoring.
Hidden Pitfall : Assuming hospitalization resolved the crisis permanently.

✅ **Study Tip for Set 5**

- Know **suicide assessment components:** ideation, plan, means, intent, protective factors.
- Practice **Crisis Response Hierarchy:** ensure safety → assess risk → stabilize → refer → document.
- Memorize **mandated reporting duties** (child, elder, dependent adult).
- Expect NCMHCE cases that test your *balance of ethics, safety, and empathy.*

Conclusion

Preparing for the NCMHCE exam requires more than just memorizing theory—it demands a strategic approach that combines clinical knowledge, practical skills, and critical thinking under pressure. Successful preparation involves understanding the exam format, practicing case simulations, honing your counseling techniques, and engaging in consistent self-assessment. By integrating study strategies, realistic practice scenarios, and a disciplined study schedule, candidates can build confidence, reduce test anxiety, and improve their ability to make sound clinical decisions in real-time. Ultimately, thorough preparation not only increases the likelihood of passing the NCMHCE but also strengthens the foundation for competent and ethical clinical practice, equipping future mental health counselors with the skills necessary to provide effective care.

Nailing the NCMHCE isn't just about knowing the material—it's about thinking like a clinician. Consistent practice, mastering case simulations, and sharpening your decision-making skills build confidence and reduce exam anxiety. With focused preparation, you're not just aiming to pass—you're preparing to provide effective, ethical care as a future mental health counselor.

Table of Contents

NCMHCE Exam Prep